To the father of
two wonderful
daughters!

Eleven Months *in* MALAYA

Eleven Months in MALAYA

September 1945 to August 1946

R.W. Holder

EDITIONS DIDIER MILLET

First published in 2005 by
Editions Didier Millet Sdn Bhd
25 Jalan Pudu Lama
50200 Kuala Lumpur
Malaysia

www.edmbooks.com

Printed and bound in Singapore
by Stamford Press Pte Ltd

ISBN 981 4155 13 6

Contents

Map of the Malay Peninsula in the 1940s

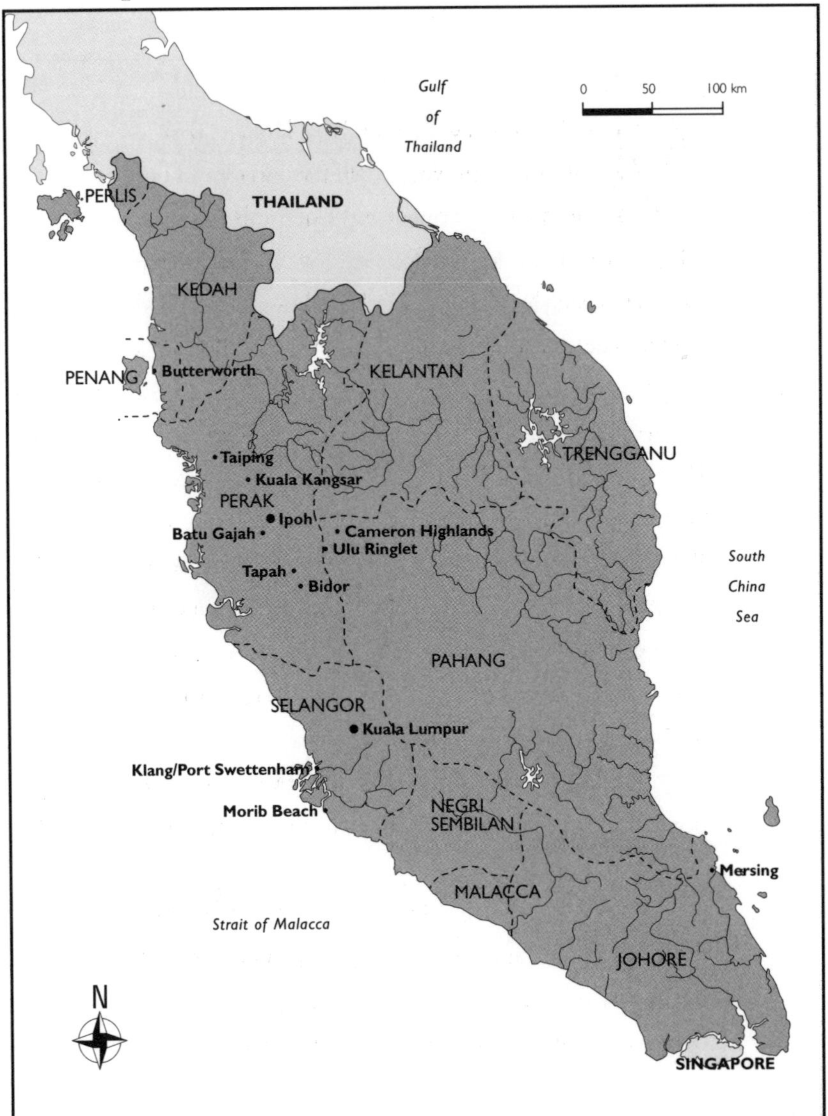

Foreword

My first recollection of Bob Holder is of a tall shadow moving down the corridor of our basement apartment at 3 Cornwall Gardens, Gloucester Road in London in 1969, clutching a suitcase in each hand. He was followed by a dishevelled young man dragging an even larger one. Bob was dropping off his son Robert who was about to share a flat with total strangers recommended to him by an HSBC friend whilst he worked out the intricacies of becoming a chartered accountant. I do not know who Bob expected to meet at the end of the corridor, but it certainly was not an Indian! Being quick of mind he immediately broke into a few words of Anglicised Hindustani as he recalled his days as a young subaltern serving in India during World War Two.

Neither of us realised then that that long walk down the corridor would result in an even longer and closer friendship.

Over the years we discovered a common trait in a voracious appetite for reading and matters historical. Several books were exchanged over far-flung continents in between numerous reunions and conversations. Besides being an astute lawyer and keen businessman, Bob is a writer of some note—this was recognised very early by none other than the great poet T.S. Eliot himself.

After I was posted by HSBC to Malaysia in November 2002, he revealed that following his stint in India he had moved, along with his regiment, to the then Malaya, where he had had some interesting experiences. I suggested he write these down as recollections of 'old Malaya'. An added bonus was to discover that Bob was a customer of our Ipoh branch in 1945–1946, and it made his request that I write the foreword an even more meaningful one!

I hope these reminiscences give readers as much pleasure in things past as no doubt Bob has had in recollecting them.

Zarir J. Cama
Kuala Lumpur
October 2004

Author's Note

In the summer of 2003, I was reunited with my fellow officers in the Royal Devon Yeomanry, those few fortunate enough to be still alive and mobile. In the months following the end of the Second World War, we had served together in Malaya and it was suggested that we should record the story about our stable of racehorses and the two meetings held in Ipoh under the auspices of the regiment. I sent a copy of the article I wrote to our old family friend, Zarir Cama, known as Zed, Group General Manager and Chief Executive Officer of the HSBC Bank Malaysia in Kuala Lumpur. Zed said the article might be of interest to the people of Malaysia and asked if I had any similar episodes to report about those unsettled times.

When I had drafted four articles, it became apparent to both of us that we were using the wrong format. I then rewrote them, and appealed to my fellow officers for more information, in particular Glyn Gabe, Greig Barr, Frank Ellen, and Desmond Mangham. What now appears owes much to their help although the errors of fact have to be attributed to me and to what can happen to one's memories over six decades. I am also grateful to them for the photographs they have supplied.

None of this would have been possible without Zed's help and enthusiasm and I take this opportunity of thanking him. I am also grateful to Alysoun Owen, who commented on the text for me, for all her advice and encouragement.

In the text I refer to Malaya rather than Malaysia. I also use other place names as they then were. Siam had changed its name to Thailand in 1938. Although in speech and print people continued to use the old name after the war, I have chosen to use Thailand.

Because of subsequent devaluation, it would be misleading to give in the text a modern equivalent in pounds sterling or American dollars to the Straits dollar issued by the British Military Administration (BMA) in 1945. There were 8.57 Straits dollars to the pound sterling, but that pound bought very much more than its diminished namesake today. One dollar, or nearly half a crown, would buy a lad four to six haircuts or a motorist three gallons of petrol. Two thousand dollars, or the proceeds of the sale of my car in Penang, was more than an agricultural worker's annual wage. Five thousand dollars, the sum for which we insured each racehorse, would buy a cottage.

I am conscious that this account of an unusual period in Malaysian history relies overly on my own memories and experiences. It all happened a long time ago.

R.W. Holder
West Monkton

1

Before the Return to Malaya

In the 19th century, the Malayan peninsula had not been the home of a unitary state. Malacca, Penang, and Singapore had been ruled by the East India Company, forming one of its four Presidencies, or administrative districts, along with Calcutta, Madras, and Bombay. When, in 1858, the territories governed by the Company were taken over by the British government, with Victoria becoming Empress of India, control of its Malayan colonies passed to the India Office. Nine years later, responsibility for their administration was handed over to the Colonial Office, and so it remained until 1941.

In the first half of the 20th century, the rest of Malaya was not, as many now assume, a British possession, but was a mixture of administrations, all acknowledging British suzerainty while still retaining degrees of independence over domestic issues. Apart from Penang, Malacca, and Singapore the country was shared between a number of independent states. Some of these states became federated under virtual British control, some had not joined the federation but acknowledged British suzerainty, and one had retained its sovereign rights, apart from that of going to war.

As elsewhere in the world, Britain had acquired control over this flourishing part of its empire through treaty and opportunism rather than conquest, and retained it through consent rather than the threat of force. Perak and Selangor in particular had, in the 19th century, been plagued with communal riots, piracy, and civil strife, in addition to periodic squabbles with their neighbours. In 1873, the British government offered to supply them (and their neighbours) with Residents, or senior British officials, who would give advice to the Head of State on all matters except those relating to religion or custom, and who would intercede in both internal and external disputes to deter the fighting and instability. As the Resident had the resources and prestige of the British Empire behind him, his 'advice' was not to be lightly disregarded. After seeing the system in operation, first Negri Sembilan, the 'Seventh State', and then Pahang also invited the British to appoint a Resident, their status becoming the same as Perak and Selangor. The hereditary rulers of other states never accepted such direct British control and Johore in particular retained its independence until 1942.

In 1909, in return for a loan to build a railway from Bangkok to the Malayan border, Thailand ceded suzerainty to the British over Kelantan, Kedah, Perlis, and Trengganu, and through that deal these states also became part of Malaya. Thus in 1941, the peninsula's territories enjoyed four different systems of government—the crown colonies ruled directly from London, the federated states with British Residents supervising policy, the states which accepted British suzerainty but ruled themselves, and Johore, whose principal concession to the British was that the Sultan would not go to war without their consent. In return for its rights over the states and substantial economic advantages, Britain undertook responsibility for their defence. Apart from the Malay Regiment recruited from local inhabitants and from expatriate British, the main military resources were the navy with its great naval base at Singapore, where the guns pointed seawards to repel invaders, and, in 1941, the British, Indian, and Australian troops who were stationed on the mainland.

Britain went to war with Germany on 3 September 1939. Following the fall of France in the summer of 1940, Japan formally aligned itself with Germany and Italy in a Tripartite Pact. There were in Tokyo many who resented the colonial possessions of the Europeans and North Americans in South-East Asia and in the Pacific. They also coveted the resources of these countries, and not least the tin and latex of which Malaya was a leading producer. Elsewhere, in Indonesia and Burma, there were oil, bauxite, and other minerals. Everywhere could be found strong agricultural economies with surpluses of rice and wood for export to Japan. With Holland also under German occupation and Britain isolated and facing defeat, the hawks in Tokyo, having conquered Korea, Manchuria, and much of China, decided that the time had come to strike further afield. Their soldiers were both fanatical and experienced. In October 1941, the bellicose General Tojo replaced the wiser Prince Konoye, a Prime Minister who favoured negotiation, especially with the United States. War with America and Britain became inevitable.

Only two problems remained: how to eliminate the American fleet in Honolulu and how to provide air cover for the invasion of Malaya. The British provided the answer to one, and the French the answer to the other.

When Italy entered the war on the side of Germany in the summer of 1940, her fleet had threatened Britain with loss of control of the Mediterranean. That in turn could have led to the loss of the Middle East and its oil. On 11 November 1940, the British Fleet Air Arm attacked the capital ships of the Italian fleet as they lay at anchor in Taranto. In the single raid with only twenty-one torpedo bombers, they sank three battleships and changed the balance of regional naval power. The Japanese naval attaché in Rome at once visited Taranto to view the wreckage for himself, and reported to Tokyo on the effectiveness of this new form of warfare.

If the Japanese High Command learned from Taranto, the American Admiral Kimmel in Hawaii did not. He continued to anchor his ships side-by-side in port at their base in Pearl Harbor, especially over the weekend when many of the crew were given shore leave. On 7 December 1940, 360 Japanese aircraft attacked the fleet and other installations at Pearl Harbor without a declaration of war. They sank or damaged all eight battleships and fourteen smaller vessels. They also destroyed or badly damaged 259 American combat aircraft. The cost to the attackers was twenty-nine aircraft.

The provision of air cover for the invasion of Malaya was

more easily, if less dramatically, solved. On 23 July 1941, Marshal Pétain, the President of France and erstwhile ally of the British, granted the Japanese unrestricted use of the military facilities in French Indo-China—Vietnam, Cambodia, and Laos. In November 1941, the Japanese army built an airfield on Phuket Island in fifteen days, within range for the provision of air cover for the invasion of Malaya. The navy had already established a base in the magnificent harbour of Camranh Bay and it was from there, and from Hainan, that the invasion fleet set out for Kota Bharu in Kelantan, their landing planned to coincide with the attack on Pearl Harbor. Again no declaration of war was made to give warning to those under attack. Indeed so timid were the British commanders about offending the Japanese that an order was issued not to attack the invasion fleet until it entered territorial waters, by which time of course it was too late. Two British battleships, the *Prince of Wales* and the *Repulse*, were all that prevented the Japanese from supporting and reinforcing their invasion. Both were sunk by air attacks on 10 December 1941.

This is not the place to dwell on the incompetence, pusillanimous leadership, and other factors which, between December 1941 and February 1942, enabled a smaller Japanese army to conquer the Malay peninsula and secure the capitulation of its more numerous opponents in Singapore. If the guns on the island fortress were looking the wrong way, so too were the military commanders, who failed to envisage a three-pronged attack from the north or to take steps to counter it. But then they had probably not envisaged many others things, including the possibility that a former ally would facilitate an assault from that direction. Among the many units who acquitted themselves well in a chaotic situation, the Malay Regiment won plaudits from all, in part because of its local knowledge but also for the steadfastness of its soldiers. At the moment of surrender, reinforcements did indeed arrive for the British in Singapore, but only to march into humiliating and, for many, fatal, captivity as they left the boat.

After the fall of Singapore, the tide of Japanese conquest swept quickly through the Philippines, Burma, Sumatra, Java, and the rest of what constitutes present-day Indonesia, lapping almost to the shores of Australia, Ceylon, and Madagascar. India itself was under threat, until the tide was turned by American power, Antipodean courage, and, for the British, the gallantry and professionalism of the predominantly Indian 14th Army under General Sir William (Bill) Slim.

By 6 May 1944, the Japanese were everywhere in retreat. Rangoon fell to the British after attack from the north combined with an amphibious assault and General Slim was able to turn his attention to the recovery of Malaya.

2

A Dry Landing on Morib Beach

The operation, code-named Zipper, involved landing two divisions of 34 Corps of the 14th Army on Morib Beach on the west coast. One of the units involved was the 25th Indian Division which included a British field artillery regiment, the 96th (Royal Devon Yeomanry), a territorial unit raised in South Devon, although, after five years, much diluted in its West Country character. The regiment had had a frustrating war, being stationed for a while in Northern Ireland, and then not being called into action after waiting on stand-by to join the Normandy battles. Its frustration had been to some extent relieved in the summer of 1944 by an involvement in manning a camp on the English Sussex coast designed to receive the traumatized French victims of the fighting around the Normandy beach-heads. As it happened no victims ever appeared at the camp, apart from a goat, but those from the regiment who were involved cherished fond memories of the nurses and other young women who also took part in the operation. Indeed, Frank Ellen, whose drawings adorn these pages, was so fortunate as to marry one of them.

I had joined the regiment in the autumn of 1944 and, as a lieutenant, was troop leader of Charlie Troop in 382 (Totnes) Battery. There were three batteries in a regiment, and each battery consisted of two troops. Each troop had four 25-pounder guns, the individual gun crews being commanded by a sergeant. A troop leader had to see that the guns arrived where and when they were expected to be, and then carry out any duties which were not specifically allocated to his seniors, the gun position officer and the troop commander. The most junior officer in the hierarchy, a troop leader, for all his title, was something of a dogsbody or gopher, and as the youngest troop leader in the regiment, my name was usually the first out of the hat when some unusual or tedious duty arose.

My story begins with the loading in Madras of the cargo ship which was to carry the regiment's guns, vehicles, and other hardware to Morib Beach on Malaya's west coast, along with two Sherman tanks, all the drivers, and some 200 Indian infantrymen. This vessel was due to leave several days ahead of the ship on which the rest of the regiment was being transported. When we had carried out a practice landing a few weeks earlier in India on the beach at Cocanada after embarking in Vizagapatam, I had been put in charge of one of the two contingents involved, sailing on the largest of the vessels used on these assaults, a landing ship (tank). I doubt if I would have been given the greater responsibility of being the only officer on the ship carrying all the guns and vehicles of the regiment to Malaya, had it not been for a tragic accident.

Late in July 1945, I had been sent with three trucks from Madras to Bangalore to pick up items of equipment needed to replace what was missing or unserviceable. It was a day's drive each way over unmetalled, corrugated roads, and the drivers and I stayed overnight in Bangalore, enjoying a good supper together in the Huan Nan Restaurant. On the way back we stopped in the wide main street of an Indian town to eat some tasty sandwiches I had had the Huan Nan prepare for us, British army field rations being unappetizing. I was standing a foot or two into the roadway and my driver was leaning against the cab door when we were hit by a truck going the other way. I was knocked down and passed under both axles of our vehicle, sustaining no more damage than a bruised shoulder. My companion's chest was crushed and he died before I could get medical help. While I was attending to the dying man, the other drivers apprehended the miscreants, who had been towing one truck backwards on all four wheels behind another, so that it swung across the road like a pendulum. In due course, they were charged with manslaughter and I was put in charge of the regimental advance party to get me out of India before I received a witness summons.

Operation Zipper had been planned for October 1945, to follow an attack on Thailand's Phuket Island, about which there is to this day some mystery. When the Phuket operation failed or was called off, Zipper was brought forward by two months. We sailed from Madras just after the second atomic bomb had been dropped on the Japanese city of Nagasaki on 9 August 1945 and then steamed around the ocean for nearly four weeks because the Supreme Commander of the Allied Forces, General Douglas MacArthur, would not allow any reoccupation of former colonial territories until he personally had taken the surrender of the Japanese on the *USS Missouri* in Tokyo Bay. We arrived off Morib on 9 September and started transferring the jeeps, trucks, tractors, guns, and limbers (trailers carrying ammunition) into the smaller landing craft which ferried them to the beach. The waterproofed vehicles drove ashore through some four feet of surf. I had no radio contact with Frank Bedder, my opposite number on the beach, and went ashore with one load to find out what was happening. There had been rumours that, despite the Emperor's announcement, the Japanese commander in Singapore, the self-styled 'Tiger of Malaya', intended to fight on. It was only when I spoke to Frank that I knew for sure that the landing had been unopposed.

I had got to know the younger ship's officers while we were killing time on the ocean. They proudly showed me an Opel Kapitän two-door six-cylinder coupé which they had hidden in a coal hold after being involved in carrying German military equipment from Crete to Piraeus in Greece. They had used the car in Madras until the police asked how it was that a field-grey left-hand-drive car with an SS pennant was roaming the city without a taxation certificate or insurance. Having managed to get the car back to the docks, the captain had told them they must dump it in the sea before they went near Madras again. This seemed a waste of what was a fine car, fairly new as it had been manufactured in 1942, and they were happy to give it to me if I could get it ashore.

Unfortunately, unlike our military vehicles, the Opel had not been waterproofed to drive through the sea. Once I knew that the landing was unopposed, and therefore the urgency less, I suggested to the commander of a landing craft that for my last load I would like a dry landing—one where the landing craft beaches and waits for the tide to go out—because, I told him, I wasn't too happy about the waterproofing of the Sherman tanks. Having been ferrying kit ashore non-stop for thirty-six hours, the navy was only too happy to oblige.

I put a fitter, Bombardier Twentyman, in charge of the Opel. On the drive up to Kuala Lumpur, a rear spring broke, and he effected a temporary repair by inserting a tyre lever among the steel leaves. He was fortunate within a few days to find, among the many abandoned vehicles on the streets of Kuala Lumpur, a Willys car of which the unusually long leaf springs fitted the Opel. In a Japanese supply depot, he liberated three new tyres and, thus equipped, the car became a general runabout for me and my brother officers, resplendent with regimental flashes on the wing, a new coat of paint to hide the German field-grey, and the SS pennant removed from the mudguard.

The journey to Kuala Lumpur with the last of my battery's vehicles to come ashore was uneventful. In each of the villages, we were watched by groups of Chinese wearing military uniform of a sort and a red star on their caps, these being members of the Malayan People's Anti-Japanese Army

(MPAJA). If the populace in general was happy to see us, they proved adept at concealing their emotions, but perhaps some of them had greeted the first arrivals with greater enthusiasm. By that evening all the vehicles for which I had been responsible had been safely delivered (bar one tractor, limber, and gun we had lost). My battery had found a comfortable billet on the Kuala Lumpur racecourse, where the Petronas Towers now stand, and I became a lowly troop leader again, until the next non-routine job came up.

For the next three or four days, men from the battery patrolled the city in vehicles or on foot, having no problems with looters despite the absence of any civil authority. Any policeman who would not collaborate with the Japanese was long gone, and those who had collaborated with them had every reason to make themselves scarce. There was virtually no civilian traffic on the roads, although there were many abandoned vehicles, often standing in the roadway where they had run out of fuel. While Bombardier Twentyman was fixing the spring problem of the Opel, I borrowed an Austin Ten for a couple of days, filled the tank with petrol, and, when we moved north, left it by the kerb where I had found it.

Even where a store had stock, we had no money with which to buy anything, other than Indian rupees which shopkeepers didn't want. This was because, in the interregnum between the surrender and our arrival, the MPAJA had got their hands on large amounts of the Japanese occupation currency, which they had earmarked for financing their revolution. The British countered this by declaring the currency worthless. For a couple of weeks or more, the authorities had nothing to put in its place. As soon as Indian infantry regiments arrived in the city, we left Kuala Lumpur, drove north, and came to rest in Bidor.

It is of course impossible to say how the Morib landing would have gone if the Japanese had not surrendered, although it has been a matter of much speculation since. General Slim was confident that the operation would have succeeded, and his confidence in his 14th Army was never misplaced. Certainly the MPAJA, under the guidance of its minders from the British Force 136, as the Special Operations Executive which supplied the infiltration teams was known, would have cut the railway and hampered the Japanese movement of reinforcements by road. Apart from the hazards implicit in any sea-borne landing, the significant weakness in the Morib plan was that there was only one good road leading away from the beach.

We now know that no more than one battalion of Japanese troops, about 1,000 men, was stationed near enough to react immediately to the landings, their main strength being in Kedah where they had expected the invasion to take place. At Morib there were none of the complex defensive positions which faced the Allied Forces landing in Normandy in June 1944, and our landing was supported by a massive force of twenty-one warships, whose fire would have been brought to bear on the defenders, as would that from 180 naval aircraft. There was, as the critics point out, a sandbar offshore which the largest landing craft could not clear at low tide, as there had also been at Cocanada, where our invasion rehearsal took place. That is why our equipment was ferried ashore in smaller landing craft than the landing craft tanks which were used at Cocanada, one of which had became stuck off its beach and never made it to the shore. (Happily, the battery for which I was responsible was in the other one.) That is why you hold dress rehearsals.

Those who maintain Morib would have been a disaster if we had met Japanese resistance also contend that the flooding of the road behind the beach would have hampered the operation. The landings did indeed take place at the time of the highest tides, the road did flood, and Frank Bedder had been soaked in his sleeping bag by seawater as he slept on top of the dunes waiting for the guns to arrive. However, the lateral road was not important as there was an exit from the beach opposite the route inland which meant that the vehicles did not have to use the flooded road running behind the beach, and in any case the floods drained when the tide went down.

A report on the landing from 224 Group of the Royal Air Force referred to 'vehicles drowning in scores' and 'ditched tanks which tore up the road surfaces and grass verges'. Some vehicles had to be winched out of the sea after stalling in the surf but, with just one exception that I know of, they were not lost and, as for the tanks, if one was 'ditched' it would have been immobile, not tearing up road surfaces. Certainly when I drove away from the beach I saw no trail of abandoned 14th-Army vehicles, and the road inland to Klang remained passable even for a late arrival such as the Opel, which had tyres bald of tread and no four-wheel drive. The RAF report continued, 'A lack of vehicles ashore made the movement of stores impossible', a point also made by those who say that the decision to use Japanese trucks to speed up movement inland was another indication of failure. If the critical airmen, and other absentees, had taken part in an assault landing, they might have understood that the first vehicles you need ashore are bulldozers if there are fixed defences, and a truck with a powerful winch to pull any stalled vehicles out of the sea. Tanks and guns are landed next. Other transport comes last because the troops will not be in a position to drive around and move stores inland by road until the beachhead has been secured. For the Morib landing, those who did the operational planning cannot be condemned for not having anticipated a clear and unimpeded run by road to Kuala Lumpur.

These myths are still doing the rounds. In 2002, a retired army officer was holding forth about Operation Zipper in my presence and maintaining that the invasion would have been a disaster because all the guns had been lost in the surf owing to the soft sand. They, along with most of the vehicles, he told us, had failed to get ashore. His information came from an impeccable source, an uncle who had been a brigadier on the Staff thousands of miles away in Colombo, Ceylon. He was not best pleased when I told him that I had been rather closer to the scene than his uncle and had witnessed the entire operation from a vessel anchored under a mile offshore. We had indeed lost the one 25-pounder gun when the tractor stalled and another landing craft settled on top of it before the tractor, limber, and gun could be winched out of the sea. But that was all. And, I added, we also managed to land two Shermans and a German staff car.

As for the Opel, when the regiment became based in Ipoh towards the end of 1945, the car came with us. Spare parts generally proved not to be a problem because its General Motors engine was almost identical to those in our American-built Chevrolet gun tractors. The badly worn graphite clutch plate was however non-standard. Fortunately my good friend, Artificer Sergeant Major Major, who commanded our Light Aid Detachment (the regimental workshop), was at that time helping with overdue maintenance at the Perak hydroelectric depot, where he discovered in the store a block of graphite from which he was able to machine a new clutch plate. The Opel's brakes were awful, but we had to live with that.

Early in 1946, military personnel were ordered to hand over to the Custodian of Enemy Property all vehicles acquired in Burma, Thailand, Indo-China, Indonesia, or Malaya. Having by then lost confidence in the integrity of the Custodian's department after an incident involving two Leica cameras, as will appear shortly, it seemed unfair once more to put temptation in his way. When my commanding officer sent for me and asked why I had not handed over my car, I pointed out that the order did not apply to me, as I had acquired it on the high seas. 'You should be a lawyer,' he said. However by July, with demobilization looming, I had to get rid of the car. I could not find anyone prepared to register it in Ipoh, where a returned British official, under whose authority such matters came, took a view of regulations, protocol, and perhaps too his own importance, which differed from that of those of us who had seen service with one West African and three Indian Divisions and learned that common sense is often preferable to going by the book. I therefore resolved to take the car to Penang, where I knew someone who could help me sell it. Disaster nearly struck when I drove on to the ferry from Butterworth, and found my brigadier on board. In so confined a space it was inevitable that he would see me. I avoided him as best I could, sold the car for $2,000 (Straits) in cash, and returned to Ipoh to face the music. As expected, my colonel summoned me to his office to ask me why I had not talked to the brigadier. 'Because,' I said, 'he was with a lady whom I knew not to be his wife.' 'Excellent answer,' replied the colonel and he left it at that.

3

A Disarming Experience

One of the first officers from the Royal Devon Yeomanry to be ferried ashore at Morib was Glyn Gabe, who had been given the task of controlling fire from warships directed at Japanese land forces and with it the imposing title of Forward Observation Bombardment Officer. Clearly his means of communication from the shore with those afloat were superior to mine afloat with those ashore. He did not at least have to take a swim to find out what was happening as I had to. After being carried shoreward by an amphibious DUKW (or Duck) and making his way inland on foot, Glyn came across an abandoned vehicle in working order and, having no targets to attack, drove with his two gunners to Port Swettenham (now known as Port Klang), twenty-five miles from Morib beach, where they found Japanese officers in the police station waiting to surrender. The Royal Navy had already arrived in the port and so, after taking possession of a sporting gun for his personal use, Glyn and his companions left the officers to the sailors and moved up country, meeting other groups of Japanese on the way looking for someone to take them prisoner.

His experience was replicated by others from the regiment as they left the beach, with small bodies of Japanese soldiers wandering about and waiting for someone to tell them where to go. When we arrived in Bidor, a small town some forty-five miles south of Ipoh, we were told there was a larger body of

Japanese soldiers waiting for us. I'm not sure how well-informed my battery commander, David Scott, was when he ordered me to deal with them and there was no point in referring back to him when I found the task not quite as routine as he had implied. In those first extraordinary weeks, everyone had so many non-military duties thrust upon them that, once an order had been given, it was assumed that the instruction would be carried out straightaway, played by the book where possible but ignored as necessary.

The camp into which the battery moved in Bidor was on the northern edge of the town. It consisted of solid wooden huts and had a large watch-tower built out of massive timber, which the Japanese had used to observe parachute drops of British men and *materiel* in the tin tailings which abutted the site. As this scrub area led into the foothills and the jungle, none of the British soldiers in Force 136 or their helpers in the MPAJA was caught there and you got the feeling that the Japanese, cut off from their homeland for a long time by the naval blockade, had in the latter days of the war lost much of the initiative and enthusiasm which they displayed in the conquest of the peninsula.

Force 136 was a British unit formed to operate behind the enemy lines, especially to organize and arm local resistance against the Japanese. In Burma, where the Burmese were sympathetic to the Japanese and not inclined to help the 14th Army if it meant a return to British rule, Force 136 found its support among the Karens and other tribesmen living in the hills. In Malaya their local associates were almost all Chinese, a race which had suffered especially during the occupation and also one which included many communist sympathizers. With its large Chinese population and convenient topography, the area around Bidor was a focal point of Force 136 and MPAJA activities. Amazingly, Force 136 only lost one man in Malaya and then not by enemy action. An unlucky parachutist landed in a lake and was unable to disentangle himself from his gear before drowning. The benefits from the Force 136 operation were not limited to sabotage and to potentially harassing the Japanese army as the sea-borne troops came ashore. By working and living with the MPAJA, they learned who their leaders were and what were their plans after the Japanese had been evicted. They also knew the location of the MPAJA's camps in the jungle, and of its arms caches.

The one evening I had in camp immediately after we arrived at Bidor, before being sent to deal with the Japanese, was fascinating because three members of Force 136 gave us a briefing on the political situation, both locally and in the country as a whole. No politician, British or Malay, should have claimed later that what became known as 'the Emergency' took them by surprise. Some of the actions we took in the hope of avoiding a civil conflict, which were later disavowed by Whitehall and Westminster, may have been short on legality, but they were long on effectiveness. That effectiveness would have been diminished, economic recovery delayed, and human suffering increased, had our conduct been constrained by the presence of 'embedded' television reporters or of a war correspondent as is that of present-day peacekeepers. Respect for the law is great when both sides play by the rules. However you cannot win at soccer if you only use your feet when your opponent picks up the ball and runs. We did not have to wait to be shot before disarming a dissident.

The briefing by the men of Force 136 was all the more valuable because we were sadly ignorant about the country in which we found ourselves. The logic behind not telling soldiers anything about the place they are going to invade must be that to do so would breach security, although it could hardly have been thought that the troops gathering in Madras and Rangoon were destined for anywhere but Malaya. Instead of learning about the politics, religions, and geography of the Malay peninsula, all the lectures we had in India in the summer of 1945 from the earnest, bespectacled officers of the Army Bureau of Current Affairs were to the effect that after the war, the poor would become rich and the rich poor, unless imperialists such as Winston Churchill remained in power. If that were to happen, the army's demobilization would be postponed indefinitely, as, they told us, had happened in 1918. In the British general election that summer, the men in Charlie Troop were not taken in by the promises of future wealth, but they did want to go home, and marked their ballot papers accordingly, apart from those who like me were too young to have a vote because we were not yet twenty-one. Given the political slant of the lectures to us on current affairs and the overwhelming desire of conscripts to get home as soon as possible, none of us had been surprised by Labour's landslide victory in the general election held in July 1945.

The morning after our arrival in Bidor I was ordered to get a squad together and take charge of the Japanese in a camp about three miles away, to the south-west of the town. We were to strip them of everything but a change of clothing and then march them to Bidor station, several miles away, where they would be taken by train for repatriation from Singapore. I would need to get on with it, I was told, before their food ran out. It sounded simple enough, but I had the good sense to take with me my old partner, Sergeant Peasey, in case things turned out differently from what my battery commander suggested. In my army experience generally, and especially with this kind of job, they often did.

Sergeant Peasey came from a family of butchers to which trade he had been apprenticed when he was called-up and, in his mid-twenties, was one of our older and more experienced soldiers. He had also been useful to have around when our meat ration was delivered on the hoof. When we arrived in Bombay, some eight months earlier, I had been sent ashore ahead of the regiment with instructions to locate our guns and equipment, which had been sent out from Liverpool in a separate ship, and take them down to Bangalore by train. I will not weary you with our adventures in the city, or even tell you about the row I had when an Indian swimming bath attendant tried to prevent one of my gunners, who was of African descent, from joining the rest of us in the pool. Suffice to say that Sergeant Peasey and a small squad under him had travelled on the cargo boat, having a more comfortable ride than the rest of us on the *Otranto*, a liner converted into a troop-ship. He took charge of me rather than the converse and thanks to him, every piece of equipment arrived safely in Bangalore, apart from one or two burst tyres caused by the difference in temperature between England and India. Our train trip from Bombay through Poona to Bangalore was more of an outing than a duty, especially as I spent much of the time on the footplate rather than in the uncomfortable guard's van which had been attached for our accommodation.

Sergeant Peasey was no less a stalwart in Malaya. The camp where the Japanese were waiting was at the end of a narrow track and turned out to be substantially larger than the barracks the battery was occupying on the other side of town. We expected to find a small band of men: it would be wrong to call them prisoners, because there was no security and they had been free to come and go as they pleased. Someone, possibly the MPAJA, had already removed their weapons and all officers above the rank of major had vanished. We never tried to count how many men were there but, as there were two full trainloads, there cannot have been less than a thousand of them for the fifteen of us to process.

There was a hospital in the camp and its senior medical officer, a major, had been educated in the United States and spoke fluent English. For the next ten days or so, until our 'guests' had left, I kept him close to me and in effect used him as our adjutant. We were amazed by the discipline and docility of the Japanese troops and by the understanding of basic English which many of them possessed. We had no food for them and the running of the camp remained in their hands. We started by taking batches of fifty men into a shed and making them strip and hand over all the watches and other valuables they had looted on their passage through China, Indo-China, and Malaya. By the end of the first day we had a pile of 'souvenirs', including two Leica cameras we had taken from their war correspondent, and these we duly sent back to Brigade Headquarters in Tapah as instructed, for onward transmission to the Custodian of Enemy Property, we might assume. This procedure, dutifully handing over everything we found, continued for two days. Being of a suspicious turn of mind, it was then that I inquired about the fate of the cameras, only to find that they had gone walkabout after reaching the higher echelons of command. I thereupon decided that a change of policy was required while we dealt with the rest of the Japanese.

My orders were to take charge of the 'prisoners', process them, and hand them over for repatriation. When we had a trainload ready, we contacted Brigade and marched the men to

Bidor station. The train was there but without any escort to watch over the Japanese on their journey and it hardly seemed right to entrust them to the engine driver, the fireman, and the guard. I therefore sent a message to Sergeant Peasey to carry on the processing work until I returned and I then boarded the train myself. The difficulty turned out not to be keeping the Japanese soldiers on the train but, as I had feared, keeping civilians off it and it was one of the few occasions that I had to use my revolver—the butt rather than the barrel to discourage those civilians who tried to travel with us by hanging on to the outside step of the coaches. Arriving in Singapore in the early hours after riding part of the way on the footplate and sympathizing with the fireman who had his work cut out firing the boiler with wood rather than coal, I at last found someone who was prepared to take my charges off me. I called at the Raffles Hotel for breakfast and took the next train back to Bidor.

A distressing incident at the camp illustrated the difference in attitude between those British/Indian troops who had fought in Burma and those who had not, and the stoical nature of the Japanese. Soon after we arrived there, we received a requisition for a working party of twenty prisoners from an Indian regiment which had arrived in Telok Anson. All seemed in order and so my Japanese major duly arranged it. Five days later seventeen men were returned to the camp in an appalling state, having been given the job of dredging a dry dock using empty seven-pound jam tins. Three had died. The Japanese made no comment or protest. I included details of this affair in my report when the duty was done, but heard nothing more. A verbal report was all that the battery captain, or second-in-command, needed, but a written report covered your back more securely.

For our own quarters, my team and I occupied what must have been the guardhouse complex. In it there was a room about twelve feet by ten stacked with Japanese occupation banknotes, floor to ceiling. We took a few as souvenirs but left the rest there when our job was done. Whether the MPAJA had missed them, or left them when they were declared worthless, I never discovered. In front of our billet there was an acre or more of marshy ground, with the inevitable swarms of mosquitoes. I asked the major if anything could be done about this health

hazard. Within hours, gangs of Japanese soldiers had stripped to the waist and began work, digging drainage trenches and constructing wattle panels to hold the sides. They worked by day and by night, under improvised lighting, and had drained the swamp when we left the camp after a stay of ten days or so.

It soon became obvious that we were unable to segregate those who had been searched from those who hadn't, although we continued to come down hard on the locals who arrived trying to barter valuables for food. I reached agreement with the major that we would not touch personal possessions but anything that had been looted must be surrendered. We did the occasional random check to see if anyone was flouting this rule, but they never were. The piles of watches and other goodies continued to mount, although we became more discriminating in what was sent back to Brigade. My own watch had been stolen by the navy when I swam ashore at Morib, leaving most of my clothes on the landing craft. It seemed only fair that I should replace it with a rather special chronometer. I told the lads that they could have no more than five watches each, which should be shared with discretion when we returned to the battery. Sergeant Peasey or I would adjudicate upon any more valuable items, such as gold or silver.

Among the more unusual items we collected were a monogrammed sterling silver cigarette case, which I gave to my brother, and a ceremonial sword, which I gave to one of my sisters, who used it as a poker for many years. As for myself, apart from a watch or three, I kept a French double-barrelled shotgun and a comprehensive collection of mainly Indo-Chinese stamps, with numerous hand-blocked and other overprints from the Japanese occupation. It must have been amassed by a French philatelist and, as the French in the Far East had not been interned until quite late in the war, he had continued adding to the collection until the spring of 1945. Remembering the part played by our former allies in opening the invasion route to Malaya, I did not feel inclined to try to trace the philatelist and return his property. As a boy I had collected stamps, having rather more to show for my efforts than most of my friends because my father had passed on his own collection to me. Indeed, it was from knowing the various stamps issued by the individual states that my meagre knowledge of Malaya was in part derived. I was therefore looking forward to integrating my acquisition, along with other interesting overprints I had acquired, with what would be waiting for me at home.

Unfortunately, my mother, with both her sons serving in the Far East and bearing in mind the carnage of the Great War, had not been confident that we would return and understandably did not want to have constant reminders of us if we didn't. She therefore gave away nearly all our personal belongings, along with, it would seem, my stamp collection. This loss cured me of any interest in philately and I later gave the stamps in my Malayan collection to my three eldest sons who still have them. My daughter, and a fourth son who arrived later, had to go without.

It was with some relief that I escorted the second trainload to the station, driving at the rear of the marchers in a jeep to pick up any stragglers and giving Sergeant Peasey the trip to Singapore. In fact there never were any stragglers, although that day we did pick up one soldier who died on the march. My lasting impression nearly six decades later is of the rigid discipline of the Japanese soldier, the immediate and unquestioning obedience by all ranks to an order, even one issued through a doctor by a very junior officer in the army of a recent enemy. Observing their conduct I was even more glad that the war had ended when it did.

4

A Victory Parade with a Bang

The absence of any police presence in the weeks after we landed might have been expected to lead to widespread lawlessness and looting. That this did not happen can be attributed largely to the speed with which the army assumed control and in part, perhaps, to the experience of the population under Japanese occupation, when crime was liable to be treated on the spot with physical injury or worse, especially if you were Chinese. One problem we faced however was the trade in drugs looted from the hospitals in Singapore which were being smuggled to Bangkok, where they could be sold at a high price. The regiment countered this by establishing road blocks between Tapah and Ipoh in places where the single highway north was difficult to bypass. These delays hardly inconvenienced other road users, of whom there were very few, especially as the smugglers invariably travelled by night. One unexpected haul during the daytime was a vast quantity of opium, about which more will be told later.

The distribution of food was another issue the regiment had to tackle. There were two problems: the absence of money with which to buy and sell anything, and the control and ownership of the warehouses where the bulk supplies were held. Getting their hands on the rationing and distribution arrangements became a political objective, with both Chinese and Malay politicians anxious to benefit from the power and kudos associated with controlling the food supply, and perhaps also to profit financially from it. Greig Barr, the regiment's commanding officer, was determined that the rationing and distribution should remain under the control of the British army to prevent any corruption, to achieve continuity of supply, and to ensure that all citizens were treated equitably. He achieved that, with people from the regiment handling the arrangements.

A shortage of legal tender anywhere has the effect of harming economic activity. Its complete absence brings trade to a halt. Cigarettes, we found, were a poor substitute for cash. Even when banknotes were printed and released, it was a long time before enough were circulating to get the economy moving again. Having rendered void the Japanese occupation money, the British authorities solved the problem of getting its replacement into circulation by sending vast sums to army units and instructing them to spend them quickly, lavishly, and on whatever they thought fit. We were especially encouraged to initiate any programme which involved the employment of people. Glyn Gabe, for example, was given the task of inspecting rubber plantations, with authority to start paying tappers and other employees even if there was no sign of any work on the estate or of latex production. There was no formal system of accounting for this money and, as far as I am aware, no instance of any officer seeking a personal benefit from it, unless you include owning racehorses or playing golf or having a comfortable billet with plenty of servants.

Glyn was the right man to carry out the job on the rubber estates because he had been trained as a surveyor. Anyone in the regiment who had a trade or profession which could help the economy get moving again was taken off military duty and in effect operated as a civilian. I have mentioned how ASM Major worked on the Perak hydroelectric premises. My battery commander, David Scott, who was a solicitor, and Gordon Samuels, who was an Oxford law student, both sat as magistrates. Our two schoolmasters were released to assist the local educational system. Others found themselves involved in the tin industry, in restoring communications, and so on. One of the many utilities which had deteriorated badly under the occupation was the drainage system, and the regiment tackled that also. The burden of carrying out civil duties fell unduly heavily on an all-British unit because our Indian colleagues were for the most part professional soldiers, without other training, whereas we were almost all civilians temporarily in uniform, with a wide variety of skills and experience.

I cannot remember what my troop commander was doing at this time, apart from *not* commanding my troop. Frank Bedder, who was next in line to him and to whom I had reported on the beach at Morib, was also not for the moment doing any soldiering. Frank was one of the greatest assets the regiment possessed in its civilian guise, being not just a chartered accountant but one who understood commerce. Seconded to the banking industry, he was mandated to get cash into circulation as fast as possible and to see that credit was freely available for businesses. My own experience of banking in Ipoh was nothing like Frank's but nonetheless satisfactory on a personal level. I wisely opened an account with the branch of the Hongkong and Shanghai Bank and it was into this account that I eventually paid the $2,000 in cash when I sold my car. The Indian army in those days required officers to use either of two other banks based in India, but I found it more convenient to do business with HSBC. I had to close the Ipoh account when I left for home and, with their usual efficiency, the bank converted what was by then quite a useful nest egg into sterling and transferred it to my English bank.

It was because Frank was working on a daily basis with HSBC and other banks in Ipoh, and the troop commander was also otherwise engaged, that I found myself in charge of Charlie Troop when it was sent up the road to Taiping to take part in what was supposed to be a routine duty, a victory parade in the town.

If medals had been awarded for taking part in victory parades, my uniform would have carried more ribbons than it did, which was in fact none as, like many ex-servicemen, I had never bothered to indent for them. My first exposure to a triumphal parade had been in the small southern Indian town of Satyamangalam, the closest habitation to the forest in which we were engaged in jungle training. It was V-E Day (the day victory in Europe was celebrated by the Allies, 8 May 1945), and eventually I found myself, with a fellow officer, in the infants' class of a school, where immaculately dressed children sang 'Rule Britannia' for us in English, under the benevolent gaze of their master. Had he but known, the conscripts who had been sent to safeguard and win back the Empire, having seen and lived in parts of it, were of one mind about the wisdom and morality of ruling other people and while we ourselves never, never would be slaves, we were equally unhappy about enslaving others. Still, the choice of song was meant well.

I also took part in a victory parade in Ipoh. We formed up on the *padang*, the large open space in the centre of the town, along with some infantry units, fired a salute, and then drove slowly with our guns down the main street, across town, and

back again. A photograph shows that there were some spectators watching the parade, but I do not recall that the pavements were thronged with cheering crowds waving the Union Jack nor that the occasion made any greater demands on us than those of ensuring that our vehicles were clean and our uniforms pressed. Whether the Raja Muda of Perak attended, and what his subjects thought about it all, remains a matter for conjecture. It was certainly not the Raja's flag, or that of the state of Perak, which was hoisted up the flagpole and which we all had to salute.

We arrived in Taiping a day or two before the ceremony there and I had no trouble in finding billets for the troop because we were relieving another unit from the regiment. Philip Shimwell, now the godfather to one of my sons, was in command, our friendship having survived an occasion when I had taken over from him a battery gun position, accepted his location on the map, and minutes later dropped a ranging round of high explosive only seventy yards or so from where Greig Barr was controlling fire from an observation post. Greig, a cultured and polite man, used language to me over the radio that I would not include in something which might end up on a family bookshelf. When he finished, I said, 'Say again, over.' 'You heard,' was his reply. All ended well when we discovered that the only feature on the map from which Philip had worked out the relative positions of the guns, the observation post, and the target, had been marked by the cartographers in the wrong place, which was not unusual with maps of jungle areas. It turned out therefore that Philip had not been at fault, and I had not been guilty of trying to exonerate myself by blaming Philip, at least not out loud. We were therefore both forgiven.

I was aware that the leader of the MPAJA had been flown to London to take part in a victory parade and been rewarded, incongruously, with the Order of the British Empire. I did not know, however, until I reached Taiping, that certain seniors among his fellow revolutionaries had been sent without trial to cool their heels in the prison there, although I learned later that others in the regiment had been involved in rounding some of them up. The communists had taken unkindly to this treatment. The prison was not under military control and, by feigning injury, they had contrived to have some small arms smuggled into the jail and had not been disarmed. The situation was being handled by a senior expatriate police officer who had been released from Changi Prison in Singapore, having suffered the brutality of the guards and the starvation diet, and had now returned to duty. He had assured Philip that he knew how to deal with these people and sort the problem out, without military help. As we were not due to relieve Philip's men until next morning, and I knew that he would have done whatever was needed, I decided to go and have a swim. I explained my absence by saying that I had to visit a Taiping pool, which wasn't a good joke then and has not improved with age.

Although it was now some weeks since the Japanese surrender, the pool and its surroundings were as they had been the day they had left, as if one of them had just come out of the water and gone to dry off. Towels and inflatable toys were still on the surround. Empty glasses stood on the poolside table. It was only when I dived in that I realized why the locals had kept away. The water, coming down from the mountains above the town, was bitterly cold. I had a stiff neck for a week.

Early next morning Philip and his men left. They had been watching the perimeter of the prison, which was the correct way to tackle the problem if the police were going to resolve it. By now the rioters seemed to have other demands than merely obtaining their personal freedom. Perhaps it would have been to better have let them go, re-enter the prison, and then pick them up again later. But that also seemed unlikely to work. In a day or so we would see the arrival of General Dempsey or Lieutenant-General Roberts, our corps commander, to take the salute, and the last thing they would want to know about was an ongoing prison riot in the town. Nor was it feasible to release any of the prisoners so that they, like their leader, could take part in our forthcoming ceremony, with or without imperial medals on their chest.

I stationed a few men around the main gate and waited. When he appeared, the senior policeman no longer appeared confident that he could resolve the impasse without our help. It seemed that overnight the communists had effectively taken over the prison and were holding the warders hostage. My impression at the time was that the policeman was inexperienced but it is more likely that his pre-war attitudes had not been adjusted to take into account the post-war realities. An expatriate official's order was no longer something the native population acted upon without question. After further comings and goings, the policeman requested our help. There didn't seem to be any point in trying to negotiate again with the rioters nor was I going to risk the lives or limbs of the stout members of Charlie Troop by assaulting the jail, the walls of which were as effective in keeping intruders out as in keeping inmates in. There was only the one gate, facing directly down a long street. Starving the prisoners out was not an option, because there were people other than the MPAJA men inside, and anyway it would take too long. I thought about storming the jail under cover of darkness, but even that was fraught with danger. The waiting game had not worked, negotiation had not worked, and so we needed to try something else.

We had been trained to handle a dangerous situation by deploying and using every means at our disposal, unlike modern soldiers faced with similar duties. A corollary to that policy is that there is no point in having weapons which an adversary thinks you are unwilling to use, nor is there any point in making threats which you are not prepared to carry out. When a final parley between the leaders of the rioters and the police led nowhere, I had my senior sergeant unlimber his gun in the roadway facing the main gate, at a distance of perhaps 150 yards, making sure that the mutineers could see what we were doing. I then issued my fire orders in as loud a voice as I could muster. The gun was loaded with its 25-pound shell of high explosive, and rammed home so that its copper band was firmly embedded in the rifling of the barrel. The cartridge, with the explosive at charge 3, the most powerful we normally used, followed the shell into the breach. The gun was aimed across open sights at the double doors of the jail. In retrospect, there was no need to use charge 3, as it would have meant nothing to the rioters, but we all make these errors of judgment from time to time in the heat of the moment. I then asked the policeman to tell the mutineers that, if they did not come out and surrender within ten minutes, we would blow the doors down. A police sergeant passed this message on to them, although I think they already knew what was afoot, and just before the deadline we saw a white flag. After it was over, the policeman remarked. 'You wouldn't have done it, of course.' 'They thought I would,' I replied. And I would have, because the shell would have burst against the door, made an awful noise and mess, and, although it would not have killed anyone, it would have given serious cause for thought. If we had loaded anti-tank, the solid shot would have passed right through the door and maimed or killed anyone in its path. By using high explosive, we would also have gained a clear view into the prison yard, making an assault or picking off the mutineers much simpler.

There was a drill for getting a live round out of a field gun which involved pushing a wooden pole with a cup on the end down the barrel and hoping that you could disengage the shell from the rifling before the wood gave way and you accidentally touched the fuse in the nose and exploded the shell. The margin for error is slim, and nothing remains to be buried of the artificer who makes a mistake. Having just lost one of my gunners in a stupid accident with a .303 rifle, I was in no mood to risk another, or indeed myself. Anyway, I needed to stay around for the victory parade.

Over the next day or so, other units arrived for the parade, and some of them had been charged with sorting out the prison riot, the Staff having once more responded to a situation which the men on the ground had already dealt with. As for Charlie Troop, I was loath to trundle through the town with a gun carrying a live round in the barrel and so, on the day of the parade, we had to content ourselves with a static four-gun salute on the lawn in front of the club, which was, I seem to recall, on rising ground overlooking the jungle. The clubhouse was the usual handsome building with a wide verandah, a bar, a dining room, and other facilities used mainly by expatriates. Charge 1, the minimum amount of cordite in the cartridge case, makes enough noise when you are firing blanks but I had to even things out with charge 3 all round. When the time came, everything went well, including the dispatch of twenty-five pounds of high explosive into the trees some 10,000 yards away, whereupon the general called me over and remarked, 'That sounded like a live round.' 'Yes, sir,' I replied, 'it was.' Nothing more was said, although I had previously seen him talking to the policeman, and he kindly sent a note to my commanding officer commenting on the smartness of my troop and our excellent march discipline. I was not altogether sure that the way I had handled the matter was correct and so, for once, I did not submit a report myself. If the general didn't want to elaborate, there seemed to be no reason why I should.

It was not long after that that orders came from London to release all the MPAJA prisoners who were being held without trial. Although they were plotting an insurrection, they did not need at that stage to take to the jungle. They were however able to prepare, through indoctrination and threats, the support among the mainly Chinese community in the towns and villages which they would need when the fighting started. Yet, even knowing all this, the army was obliged to set them free and the rest, as they say, is history.

5

Horse Sense and Racing Certainties

Although my regiment was almost entirely composed of former Territorial Army volunteers or conscripts like myself, a regular soldier was appointed as second-in-command, perhaps to keep a military eye on the amateurs around him. The first second-in-command I knew was 'Bunny' Hanwell, whose post-war posting was to Edinburgh Castle, and his address was 'Major Hanwell, Edinburgh Castle'—brief and to the point, you might think, but too complicated in 1947 for the British post office. A re-addressed letter was delivered to him marked 'Not *SS Edinburgh Castle*—try Edinburgh NB'. The Castle Line no longer carries passengers by sea between England and South Africa and it is a long time since Scotsmen allowed people to call their proud country North Britain.

The second-in-command when we arrived in Ipoh was Martin Gregson, a keen student of horseflesh and historically the right man for a yeomanry regiment to which its part-time soldiers—small farmers or 'yeomen'—would have been expected to bring their mounts when they reported for duty. Martin had in peacetime been involved in the management of point-to-point meetings, a feature of rural England in which jockeys, of whom most are amateurs, race on hunters against each other over courses laid out on farmland. He was therefore familiar with the intricacies of handicapping and the other mysteries of the racing world. This knowledge he was soon to put to our, and his own, advantage.

The Perak Turf Club in Ipoh had, before the war, been the preserve of expatriates. Despite the love of the Chinese in particular for racing and for gambling, the horses were owned by expatriate planters or administrators and no jockeys were allowed a ride other than those from Britain or Australia. When Martin Gregson discovered some forty emaciated racehorses in the club stables being looked after, with great difficulty, by their lads (and in this context a 'lad' can be of mature years), he resolved to sort the matter out. Without exception the horses' owners had disappeared, being dead or imprisoned under such conditions that they would not be around again for many months, if ever. The jockeys too had disappeared but that was no problem as the 'lads' were perfectly able to ride the horses.

The instruction to Greig Barr that the regiment should spend all the public money it could and provide employment wherever possible enabled Martin to put the stable staff on the payroll, without having to worry about the cost. Buying forage for the horses out of public funds might have been less acceptable and, with some food rationing still in force, the fodder could have been difficult to find on the open market. After studying the army's bible, *King's Regulations*, Martin worked out that each yeomanry officer was entitled to a forage ration for his horse, at a cost which came to $32 (Straits) a month. That amounted to less than three days' pay after tax even for a junior officer like me, who received Indian Army rates plus

Japanese campaign pay, in addition to hard lying allowance, three-year increment, with all being subject to minimal Indian income tax. (In my case, typical of many others, the paymaster had not realized that the Japanese campaign was over, that the Majestic Hotel in Ipoh was not uncomfortable, and that I had not yet been three years in the army.) The cost of the forage was not such a problem as its availability, and by bringing the supply under *King's Regulations*, Martin was able to authorize the regimental quartermaster, Louis Hall, to procure it.

Louis was always prepared to provide what was needed even if it meant cutting a corner or two. An example of his flexibility occurred at my twenty-first birthday party. I had not realized it was my birthday, let alone that I had come of age, until I received a wire from my parents in the early afternoon. As it was too late to do any elaborate planning, a dozen of us went to the most expensive restaurant in Ipoh, where each diner had a young lady sitting beside him to attend to his every gastronomic requirement. The meal lasted a long time, the food being washed down with plenty of drink. Our spirits fell rather when the bill arrived. None of us was carrying much cash and it had been too late in the afternoon to draw more. Louis resolved the dilemma by slipping out for twenty minutes or so, selling some rice from the regimental stores, and returning to settle the bill.

Martin Gregson needed the consent of the commanding officer, Greig Barr, for an enterprise involving the diversion of the considerable resources which would be required to organize and run a race meeting. Greig was more interested in golf than in quadrupeds and, as he recalls, 'I let Martin get on with it.' It was also necessary to obtain the approval of a brigadier, the Commander Royal Artillery, who was also based in Ipoh, the same officer who, with his mistress, was to see me on the ferry between Butterworth and Penang when I was selling the Opel. Martin was assured of the brigadier's consent when he allocated to him the second best horse, keeping the best, *Hyafusa*, for himself, and renaming it *Silver Sands*.

The other horses were distributed on a predictable basis. Anyone who was part of regimental headquarters (RHQ) did well, and the assistant adjutant, Desmond Mangham, although still only a lieutenant, received one of the better horses. Outside RHQ, the allocation went with rank, with Major Robert Hudson having a doubly or trebly favoured animal, as we will see shortly. Some of the captains, such as Glyn Gabe and Gordon Samuels, being stationed away from Ipoh, were penalized for their absence by getting poor horses, or none at all. By the time Martin got down to the subalterns, only the less-favoured mounts were on offer. Faced with a monthly drain on our resources for a nag which never looked likely to achieve anything, the lieutenants such as myself formed syndicates, with two or three sharing a horse. The only syndicate to triumph was that of Alan Maidens, Reg Ferguson, and Beverley Ditcham, whose *Edna Star*, a no-hoper if ever there was one, turned out to have star qualities. I have to confess that my interest was at such a level that I no longer recall the name of the animal whose nosebag I was helping to fill, nor whether I shared the burden with Mike Gover, John Jones, Tony Besch, or any other of my similarly disadvantaged friends. At least I never added to my losses by betting on the sorry creature.

Another small contribution was expected from the temporary owners. There was of course the possibility that a real owner might reappear and not take too kindly to what had been done to his property in his absence. We were therefore required to pay a small premium to insure each horse against injury or death to the sum of $5,000 (Straits). I was not aware that any owners reappeared while the regiment was running the stables but if they did, they must have been so grateful for our stewardship as to say nothing. The only horse to meet an untimely death was Robert Hudson's *Venture*, in circumstances which will shortly be related, and the insurers duly paid up. The practical problem of looking after the stables was solved by the presence in the regiment of Gunner Love, who had been a circus lad before being called-up. Under Martin's direction, Love handled all the training, disciplinary, and administrative side of the stables and he also proved both an expert jockey and adept in selecting his own rides.

There is no point in having racehorses without horse-races and this is where Martin Gregson excelled himself, announcing that there would be a meeting on Boxing Day, 1945, a comparatively short time after he had taken over the stables. He was faced with a considerable administrative challenge because there was nothing left of the pre-war apparatus for organizing a meeting. The Perak Turf Club existed only in name, all the staff with experience of managing, planning, and running a meeting had disappeared. The course itself was suffering from four years of neglect and needed more than just a lick of paint on the rails. There would be no problem in finding the foot soldiers within the regiment—the gate-keepers, marshals, and so on, who could be instructed in their duties on the day. Running a meeting however required more specialist skills—a handicapper, a clerk of the course, a timekeeper, and, if the venture was to be a commercial success, someone to run the Tote.

Martin kept the allocation of horses into three classes and the choice of runners for each of the six races to himself. Some of us may have raised an eyebrow when *Silver Sands* was seen to be listed in Class 2 but nobody was surprised when, on the day, he made light work of the opposition, winning by what is known in racing circles as a 'distance'.

Desmond Mangham was appointed timekeeper and Maurice Swain was clerk of the course. With respect to them both, neither task called for special skill or training. The handicapping was more onerous, and that was entrusted to my battery commander, David Scott, who was an avid racing fan, both before and after the war as I can personally attest. Back in England, I had occasion to ring him from a telephone kiosk one Saturday in 1947, when we were both civilians once more. In those days, to initiate the call, you put two pennies in a box. The operator in the local post office would then tell you how much more money to insert and then make the connection for you, at which point you would press Button A and the money would be gobbled up by the machine. Before David's phone started to ring, the village postmistress said to me, 'I can put you through if you like, Mr 'older, but you'll only get Mrs Burchel [David's housekeeper]. Mr Scott's up Newton Abbot races.' So I pressed Button B and got my tuppence back.

Frank Bedder organized and ran the Tote. He would not have been able to undertake this huge task were it not for his secondment to the local banks. As I placed my bets, I could see through the hatch the myriad skilled tellers and other bank clerks who had been working with Frank and who had come along to help him. His organization worked perfectly and the considerable profits were divided between regimental funds and local charities. Although there were no bookmakers, this was not the only gambling that day. Greig Barr recalls how he was mystified by numerous Chinese women who sat with their backs to the horses, staring fixedly at the Tote board. Apparently they were using the money they had saved from panning for tin, not to bet on the outcome of the races, but on the final digits which appeared when the Tote stopped.

Apart from Gunner Love, all the jockeys were local men. In post-war Ipoh, as far as we were concerned, there was no racial discrimantion, apart from the fact that we had only one overseas jockey anyway.

It seemed that all Ipoh came to the races that day. If the citizens were not enthused by victory parades, the regiment had on this occasion come up with an event everyone could enjoy. There were also distinguished visitors from afar, including the Army Commander, General Dempsey. In my betting, I was fortunate that David Scott marked my card, which would have resulted in a straight six winners had I paid less attention before the last race to my companion on the day, who seemed miffed that she had backed five losers and, I suppose, wanted me to share her misery. The experience on that occasion of having all the handicapper's predictions come true has done nothing to increase my confidence in the integrity of the Sport of Kings.

The first race was duly won by the timekeeper's *Dadaboy* with Gunner Love in the saddle, giving Desmond Mangham not only $850 (Straits), about £100, in prize money but the honour of leading in the first winner. Knowing Desmond as he was then and still is, I expect he had also placed a judicious bet. The sums involved may not seem great today, but £100 represented six months' wages for an artisan in England, or three months' salary for a newly qualified solicitor. As we noted, *Silver Sands* romped home in the fourth race and of course, as with Desmond Mangham and Martin Gregson, every winning owner was an officer in the regiment. That evening there were six happier and considerably richer yeomen.

Frank Ellen, who was also present that day, wrote to me

recently commenting on 'the generally generous acceptance [by the Malayan people] of our return, after leaving them so badly in the lurch in 1941/2'. It would be fair to say that Martin Gregson's organization of the race meeting, with Greig Barr's support, did more than anything else to reconcile the citizens of Ipoh, of every nationality and class, to the British soldiers who had been billeted in the town. Many of the other tasks the regiment carried out were beneficial to the security of the people and to the economy in general, but they were not done under the public gaze. The race meeting was an initiative which produced results which everyone could see and pleasure in which they could share. It was the best possible way in which the regiment could try to repay its debt to our hosts. Martin Gregson organized a second meeting in Ipoh on 16 March 1946. Due to an outbreak of the infectious disease epizoo, again only Ipoh horses raced, with Love on this occasion riding two winners. Thanks to a deluge which left part of the course flooded, the favourite in the last race fell, bringing to a halt the rest of the field, apart from *Edna Star*, who had been too far behind to become involved. That day the Ferguson syndicate netted $3,793 (Straits). Even after splitting it three ways, that was a lot of money. No wonder every time I saw Reg Ferguson he was smiling.

I was stationed in the Cameron Highlands at the time of the March meeting and was saved the duty of escorting a young woman, who would doubtless have given me bad advice, by the fact that my brother was staying with us on a week's leave and came to the races with us. There were only four seats in a jeep and my fellow officer, Neil McGill, claimed two of them for himself and his lady companion. Nobody marked my card on this occasion and my judgement of horseflesh proved abysmal. But nonetheless it was a great day out.

At Easter 1946, the authorities in Kuala Lumpur at last got round to arranging a meeting themselves on the site of our first quarters in the city. I am almost sure that no army units had become involved with racehorses in the way that we had. In any event, by then some of those who had been imprisoned were returning to see if they could take up their former lives and claim their assets. Martin Gregson decided that he would send down only one horse from Ipoh for each of the six races. I had no interest in any of those selected to travel and in any case was not so keen on racing as to make the trip south. Someone had to stay behind and be available for duty. The result was something of a farce. The sleek Ipoh horses won the first two races by a distance and by the third the bookies, who were there in force, had stopped taking any bets on the winners. Robert Hudson's *Venture* was one of the Ipoh runners and, having won its race, it dropped dead at the post, providing Robert not only with his prize money but also with the $5,000 (Straits) insurance.

By April 1946, the officers who had been paying for the forage were being demobilized, planters and officials were returning, and it was time to hand the Perak Turf Club back to its rightful owners. Martin Gregson, with the help especially of Gunner Love, had brought off one of those rare coups where there were many winners and no losers. Not the least important factor was that half-starved animals had been cared for. The race meetings had formed an important link between the regiment and the local community. Local people had had two great days out. Individual officers in the regiment were better off, and some of them much better off, as a result of their 'ownership', while local charities and regimental funds had also benefited.

After his retirement from the army, Martin Gregson became well known in racing circles, and especially among west-country point-to-points. David Scott continued to be unavailable on days when there were meetings at Newton Abbot. Glyn Gabe had the distinction of laying out the course for the first post-war Badminton Horse Trials. I regret I don't know what became of Gunner Love, but he also should be remembered for his part in the success of this unusual army initiative, for which I personally am unable to claim any credit whatever.

6

How the British Military Administration Worked

During the interregnum between the surrender and the arrival of the British/Indian army, order of a sort must have been maintained in Malaya by the continued presence of the Japanese troops. This dangerous period for the peninsula lasted from the Emperor's elliptical message to his armies on 16 August 1945 saying that things had not turned out quite as he would have wished, until the landing at Morib on 9 September. Marines and other special forces had arrived in Penang and Singapore earlier, on 3 and 5 September respectively. The principal object of the communists in the MPAJA when they emerged from the jungle was to seize power before the British arrived and, as we noted above, they collected vast amounts of currency to finance their campaign, only to have it declared worthless. In the three weeks during which their activities went unchecked, they acted ruthlessly against their perceived opponents, held summary trials, or none, and executed over 2,500 Malayans of different races.

Despite MacArthur's order that no troops in the Far East should retake possession of former colonial territories (in which category Malaya was incorrectly included) until he had had his moment of glory in Tokyo Bay, General Slim caused doctors and medical supplies to be dropped on the camps where European prisoners were confined. Even when they were released, these prisoners were in no condition to resume any administrative role, nor were any arrangements in place for their swift evacuation. With regard to the landings, Slim's hands had been tied by the acquiescence of his superior, Lord Mountbatten, to placing the 14th Army under the orders of the American Supreme Commander. As all the arrangements had been made for the sea-borne invasion and the operation had already been launched, Slim decided to carry it out as planned rather than try to untangle the mass of men and *materiel* in place.

The MPAJA was officially stood down by the British the day we arrived in Kuala Lumpur, although, lingering long after its raison d'être had disappeared, it was not finally dissolved until 1 December 1945 when each man was supposed to hand in his gun and received a gratuity of $350. By then, many of the weapons had been cached in the jungle, along with other supplies. As ever, the foot soldiers did badly because the Communist Party appropriated most of their cash to finance its subversive operations. So long as its leaders had been confined in Taiping, other than the one receiving an imperial medal from King George VI, the communists' ability to organize support, especially among the Chinese community, was limited. From December 1945 onwards, the position was much changed, and, as regards the population as a whole, for the worse.

In other territories which the British and Americans conquered or re-occupied, the soldiers were normally able to count on the availability of trained civilians following in their wake to take over the civil administration without any interim period. Why that was not the case in Malaya is unclear, unless the suddenness of the Japanese collapse took those responsible by surprise. For whatever cause, from September 1945 to April 1946 the army was given the responsibility for security and policing as well as for getting the economy moving, thus gaining time for officials to be recruited, police trained, magistrates appointed, and those expatriate administrators who were able and willing to return to recover their health after their confinement. During these months, the source of government was named the British Military Administration.

Late in November the headquarters of the Royal Devon Yeomanry (RDY) moved to Ipoh to relieve another unit which was said to have suffered unacceptable casualties from an excessive fondness for the less reputable ladies of the town. Two of the three RDY batteries were stationed there, the third being located in Kuala Kangsar. By this time, those with specialist training or skills had been seconded to civilian work, and the commanding officer, Greig Barr, had delegated other senior officers to handle such matters as transport, rationing, and the control of food supplies. This left the subalterns, who had no relevant skills or experience, to carry out the more menial and routine task of policing and, being in this category, I was instructed to patrol a triangle of land of which two corners rested on Batu Gajah and Ipoh itself. This comprised an area of some sixty square miles, including several villages, rubber plantations, and other cultivated land. Our instructions were to prevent looting, arrest criminals, and generally keep the peace.

Because my superior officer in the troop was doing something more useful elsewhere, I was left during this time to my own devices, never quite sure how far my writ ran. The only time I had the honour of showing my battery commander, David Scott, what we were doing, some unkind person took a pot shot at us and made a neat bullet hole in one of the tyres of our 15-hundredweight truck. When that happened, it was better to drive on and ruin the tyre than stop and be shot at a second time. The incident was unfortunate because it gave David quite a wrong impression of the general quietness and security in our district.

I rarely entered the town of Batu Gajah, where an Indian infantry regiment was stationed and, I hoped, knew what was going on there. The only occasion I can recall meeting this unit was on the hockey field where, to our joint surprise, we beat them on their hard pitch by one goal to nil. I don't think I would have been popular if I had returned. Indians are meant to be better at hockey than Europeans.

The troop had about fifty men available for this duty, none of them any better trained than I was. We were given no rules of engagement or any advice as to what weapons we should carry. The intelligence with which we were provided was minimal, especially with regard to any political subversion. We had no interpreters, and my attempts to use my basic Malay only elicited a response when the person I was addressing wanted to understand me. My Urdu, equally inadequate and with its verbs confined to the imperative case, was incomprehensible to the Tamil workers on the rubber plantations, while the shopkeepers of Indian descent were usually unhelpful if not antagonistic, and tended to lose their command of English in our presence.

We had to deal with local inhabitants of three different races, or four if you divide the Tamil rubber tappers from the other Indian shopkeepers, and each of them had a different attitude towards us. The Malays, about whom we were perhaps wrongly warned to be wary as some of them were said to have collaborated with the Japanese, seemed to accept, or even welcome, our presence when we were seen to be doing no more than keep the peace. In my view, any suggestion that the Malay people were in any way untrustworthy was quite unfounded: nobody could blame them if they had opted for a non-confrontational approach with the Japanese. The Chinese were initially the most friendly, having been persecuted by the Japanese, and for a while were generally helpful. The workers on the rubber estates, mainly Tamils, seemed to adopt a neutral attitude towards us. The only overt animosity came from the Indian shopkeepers, some of whom still displayed a picture in their shop windows of Subhas Chandra Bose, the head of a puppet Provisional Government of Free India, and responsible for raising from prisoners-of-war and local volunteers the Japanese-controlled Indian National Army. Because of their understandable desire for Indian freedom, most of these traders seem to have been supportive of the Japanese during the occupation.

While we may have thought the Bose supporters misguided, our practice was not to pay much attention to any display which might have been thought provocative. Bose was dead, the Indian National Army no longer existed, and Indian independence was a matter of time. As it was a long time ago and many myths have since been woven round Bose and his army, it may help to record here how we saw things at the time. The Jiffs, or members of the Indian National Army, were mainly recruited from soldiers who had been captured by the Japanese and then, in many cases, been induced to switch sides through appalling ill-treatment if they refused. They had also witnessed the debacle of the fall of Malaya, Singapore, and then Burma, destroying the aura of impregnability of British imperialism, just as the Crimean War created a similar impression of British vulnerability and weakness before the tragic events of 1857 in India. The subsequent British victories in Burma, including those at Kohima and Imphal, had for the most part been won, and the invasion of Malaya undertaken, by Indian divisions, composed of men who had volunteered for service, albeit often under economic pressure, and had pledged their loyalty to British India without in any way renouncing their wish for independence. While we British pitied the Jiffs, our Indian colleagues despised them. Wisely, the Japanese seldom used the Jiffs as fighting troops, and when they did, the Jiffs normally surrendered as soon as they could to their compatriots, who no less keenly wanted a free India, but not one subject to Japanese patronage.

Like much else, the rubber plantations in our patch had been neglected for four years. A lot of the ground showed secondary growth, mature trees had not been tapped, and managers were only slowly returning. Other cultivated areas did not require so much of our attention as there were people working there and there was less worth stealing. It was impossible for us to guard everything but, by sending out teams of four men under a sergeant or bombardier in jeeps or 15-hundredweight trucks, we were able to keep an eye on things and, more importantly, to be seen doing it. I had no compunction about our using force so long as we never shot anyone. For my own part, I was so inaccurate with a revolver that I was worried that, if I had to use it, I would hit someone when trying to miss. I therefore took with me on these outings a Sten gun with the stock removed, so forming a stubby and light sub-machine gun capable of firing bursts of up to thirty rounds if you didn't try to get an extra bullet or two in the magazine. It was quite safe to remove the stock so long as the spring holding the bolt in place was properly adjusted. By having one round in four tracer, a burst not only made an infernal noise but the pyrotechnics were impressive, especially at night time. I also had a shrewd idea where the rounds were likely to land.

There were no typical incidents in this type of patrolling and being shot at only happened the once. From time to time we went on foot and recovered looted property from shops, including a surprising number of tyres from army vehicles, which seemed to be in special demand. On these occasions, we merely confiscated the illegal goods without laying any charges. The dumps of latex by the roadside, which the Japanese had been unable to ship because of the Allied blockade, had been stolen by then. The one large-scale crime we came across related to a stockpile of tin in a large warehouse which, regrettably, had been appropriated and sold by a British officer from another unit, and turned out to have been a major theft in more than one sense. I believe the major responsible was subsequently arrested, court-martialled, and sent to prison.

An unusual incident occurred when, having detained two men who were stripping the galvanized iron off the roof of a storage shed on a rubber estate, we carelessly allowed the third to get away. There was a large pond nearby and I loosed off a few rounds from the Sten gun to let the fugitive know we were still about. To my amazement he emerged from the water, where he had been concealed while breathing through a straw. I had thought that kind of trick only happened in the cinema, just as the only people who ever manage to hit a target with a handgun are those who appear on a screen.

We were on this patch for about ten weeks before my troop had the plum posting to the Cameron Highlands. During this period I had been responsible to another troop commander, no longer Frank Bedder but Geoff Stavert, who in civilian life had been a schoolmaster. Whereas Frank the chartered accountant had spent most of his time helping bankers, his successor had been given the job of supervising various aspects of the secondary school system, where years of staff shortages and the lack of money had wrought havoc. The best way of letting Geoff and those above him know what was going on was by writing weekly reports, which also had the virtue of covering my own back. Apart from two subsequent occasions to which I will refer later, I had the feeling, with these reports, that a doubting child experiences when he sends a letter up the chimney to Santa Claus. Certainly nobody filled my stocking that Christmas.

Books written about those troubled times imply that there was something called the British Military Administration which ruled Malaya during this period and had a separate existence from the army. All I can recall is that during the weeks while my troop was engaged in this non-military duty, we saw no civilian officials or police, or anyone saying they were from a military administration. I did however note, and report, a significant change in the attitude of many people of Chinese descent to our presence—from being open and welcoming to becoming evasive or even obstructive. We knew that communists released from Taiping were active in the Ipoh area and in Batu Gajah, and that Perak was the likely place for any trouble to break out. What none of us foresaw, with our limited intelligence sources, was the extent to which the party had been recruiting for the Min Yuen underground, and the pressure being applied to Chinese people in particular not to co-operate with the British. We have to assume that, after April, when the British Military Administration came to an end, someone with greater skills and experience was there to make a better fist of it. But I wouldn't bet on it.

Greig Barr wrote to me recently about 'the performance of military units sucked into the vacuum of the absence of civil government'. He continued, 'I am surprised that more records were not kept at the time… I like to think the RDY didn't do too badly.' From a modest man and an admired commanding officer, that seems a fair judgment.

It never fell to my lot to have to pay any of the myriad workers for whom we found employment at this time, a duty which, it would seem, was not to be entrusted to those below the rank of captain. Glyn Gabe recalls how, after setting tasks for rubber tappers by clearing secondary growth, and engaging gangs for road repairs, he was also responsible for going to the bank and paying them, with the recipients giving a thumbprint by way of acknowledgement of payment. In the medley of Chinese, Malays, and Tamils—men, women, and children—there was always a shortfall whereupon it was necessary for the Gabe thumb to make up the numbers. This impressive document had then to be presented to the bank the following week, when cash would again be handed over. As Glyn remarks, it would have been easy to cheat, but so far as he knew, nobody did.

I at least learned something useful in those trying times. Many years later my smattering of Malay helped tip the balance when the Singapore government was in the market for ten police boats, and we were in final competition with a Swedish rival. The chief of police, who was a Malay, had seemed to favour Volvo, even though I pointed out to him that their test results achieved in the cold waters of the Baltic were unlikely to be replicated in the tropics. (In effect, a powerboat can go some three knots faster in cold waters.) Getting nowhere with this tack in English, I suggested, in Malay, that it was time we adjourned for a drink. On that occasion at least my message was received and understood.

7

Bench Warming

Previous chapters have referred to the lack of any police force when the British/Indian forces landed, and about the affair at the Taiping prison. Besides policing and imprisonment, there is a third leg to the stool of justice, which is the trial and sentencing of the accused. A trial requires the presence of a judge or magistrate, and there were none of those when we landed. There were however two different classes of people to be tried: the normal run of offenders against the law, and those Japanese who had committed 'war crimes', or acts which, in the eyes of the victors, were so cruel and contrary to the Geneva Convention governing the treatment of prisoners that they merited punishment. It was left to the army in general, and the regiment in particular, to provide judges for both types of court.

After their conference in Moscow in October 1943, the Allied leaders, Churchill, Roosevelt, and Stalin, announced that it was their intention to punish the principal Nazis, although they did not choose to give details of the offences with which they would be charged or the tribunal which would sit in judgment on them. As the collapse of Germany approached, British jurists questioned the validity of setting up a new court to try offences which had not been defined when they were alleged to have been committed. In the United States and the Soviet Union there were no such qualms and in May 1945, it was agreed that the trials would go ahead. On 8 August, two days after dropping the atom bomb on Hiroshima, the victorious Allies signed a charter establishing what were to become known as the Nuremberg trials. The twenty-four defendants at Nuremberg were all senior Nazis. Subsequently lesser Nazis and other defendants, not all of German origin, were charged elsewhere with numerous atrocities committed in the territories conquered by Germany, in the concentration camps, and against the Jews, gypsies, and other unfortunates not recognized as having any rights by the Nazis.

The principle having been established that the victors in war can try the vanquished for the crime of waging war against them, a tribunal similar to that in Nuremberg was established in Tokyo. The prosecution laid charges against twenty-eight Japanese who were chosen as a representative sample of those responsible for 'waging an aggressive war'. The list was as notable for those not included as for those who went on trial, Emperor Hirohito being an absentee at General MacArthur's insistence, along with two former Prime Ministers and known sadists whose conduct had affected the Chinese and Koreans rather than the British, Australians, Dutch, or Americans. Despite many of the accused pleading guilty as charged, the Dutch representative at the court opposed many of the convictions, while the French judge thought that all the cases should have been dismissed.

At least the Nazis at Nuremberg could not complain about

the quality of the judges sent to try them, or the rules of evidence which were observed. No such niceties were observed in Tokyo. The prosecution was allowed to bring diaries of victims, hearsay, unsworn statements, and similar evidence before the court, much of which was unreliable and all of which would have been rejected in a normal hearing. Those who defended the lax procedures were right when they pointed out that many of the victims were unable to give direct evidence because they were dead. They were however wrong to allow justice to be tainted by a desire for vengeance.

As in Germany, lower tribunals were established throughout the Far East to try those who had been guilty of brutality, especially those who had acted as prison guards, with Koreans and Taiwanese joining Japanese as defendants. Defendants categorized under Class B were alleged to have performed such acts personally, and those under Class C of ordering them or failing to prevent them. Four tribunals were established in Malaya, sitting in Singapore, Kuala Lumpur, Penang, and Seremban. If some of the judges in Tokyo were criticized for being insufficiently qualified for the task, those appointed for most of the regional courts were even less suitable and, as in Tokyo, their courts enforced no normal rules of evidence.

In Malaya, there were few acquittals, although many of those condemned to death had their sentences commuted to terms of imprisonment and those given lengthy terms of imprisonment had their period of confinement reduced. Despite such clemency, no less than 199 of the worst offenders were executed and another 126 were imprisoned. To what extent the accused were being judged by standards alien to their culture and laws is something to which the tribunals gave sparse attention. Even in England the desire for vengeance was such that few expressed unease about the judicial killing of the Irishman, William Joyce, also known as Lord Haw Haw, because of resentment at his wartime broadcasts from Germany. Before expressing overmuch sympathy for those who were convicted of 'war crimes', we should recall that many Japanese who committed what the Malayan people or the British would consider heinous deeds were repatriated without standing trial, and the Emperor himself retained his Fellowship of the Royal Society, the venerable British learned institution.

Asked for a candidate to sit on the tribunal in Singapore, Greig Barr decided to send Major Humphrey Smith, the commander of 381 Battery. His choice demonstrated one of the basic rules of regimental life: when a commanding officer is required to supply a candidate for a job which involves promotion for the person selected but also means that he will have to leave the unit, the officer will usually send not the most able, suitable, or deserving of his subordinates but the one he feels can best be spared. If hitherto I have given the impression that every officer in the regiment, myself excluded, was a man of ability and a gentleman, now is the time to correct any misconceptions. Major Smith had recently come out poorly in an external inspection of the regiment's efficiency and his personal conduct was exemplified by an incident over a gift to our surveyor, Glyn Gabe, to which we will refer later.

When, as the longest serving officer, Glyn was given permission to accompany Greig Barr and Gordon Samuels to Singapore to catch the boat home, he ran into the newly promoted Colonel Smith and found him to be wearing on his chest medal ribbons which had not adorned it a few weeks previously. It was not until many decades later that those of us who served with him realized what a novelist manqué had been lost when we read his obituary, which he must either have written himself or for which he had provided the material.

In Ipoh, the senior judicial post, equivalent to a judge in a normal criminal court, was taken by a solicitor-soldier from another unit called John Adams, or Hang-'em-all Adams as he was known to describe himself on occasion. He was in fact a humane and amusing man, facing a difficult task. Some of the crimes with which he had to deal were gruesome. He sat without a jury but with two assessors and on the one occasion he asked me to join him, we sentenced a violent and persistent thief to seven years in prison. The man was clearly guilty but I felt uncomfortable as an Englishman sitting in judgment on someone who had to follow the proceedings through an interpreter and hardly seemed aware of what was going on. My fellow assessor and I left John Adams to fix the length of the sentence, nodding our heads in agreement at the right moment.

The mind-set of some British officials about the future government of Malaya was highlighted by the Adams appointment. He was required to return to the United Kingdom, have himself removed from the Roll as a solicitor, and then sit his dinners so that he could be admitted to the Bar, in default of which he would not have been allowed to keep his judgeship. The concept that for the foreseeable future only those who had qualified as a barrister in England would be fit to sit as High Court judges in Malaya was, in retrospect, bizarre, and indeed seemed strange to some of us on the ground at the time. Adams had proved a competent and fair judge. A few months in England were not going to change that and he was sadly missed during his unnecessary absence.

In addition to releasing Humphrey Smith, the regiment provided two magistrates for the lower courts, sitting alternately part-time and alone, without assessors. One was David Scott, who had been practising as a solicitor at Kingsbridge in Devon before the war. The other was Gordon Samuels, who had been studying law at Oxford University. Glyn Gabe recalls how he was present in the local court, as a spectator it must be said, on the first day that Gordon Samuels presided. One of the prisoners to appear was a gentleman caught with a large quantity of opium in a bullock cart when the regiment had been on the lookout for smugglers of prescription drugs between Singapore and Bangkok. After hearing the evidence,

Gordon pronounced a guilty verdict, followed by a lecture on the return of British justice and the heinousness of the offence, which necessitated an exemplary punishment. He then imposed a huge fine. The prisoner at once produced a large wad of notes, peeled off the amount needed, and walked off, leaving a perplexed magistrate in his wake.

David Scott filled the other vacancy in Ipoh for a magistrate. He had been my troop commander at the Officer Cadet Training Unit (OCTU) and had applied for me to join the regiment when he himself was posted to it. He was in turn my battery captain, my battery commander, and my commanding officer. After the war, when I was articled at the firm he had founded, he kindly let me use his house for two months until I found my own accommodation.

One of our tasks at the fag-end of 1945, you may recall, was to find employment for the local inhabitants until the economy recovered and to get as much cash into circulation as we could. To this end we were encouraged to spend the government's money relatively freely, especially on wages. When my battery moved to Ipoh, we naturally looked for the most comfortable accommodation for ourselves and our gunners, and this proved to be the Majestic Hotel. Although on previous occasions I had been sent ahead to find camping sites or billets, on this occasion I was not involved in the choice. On the ground floor of the hotel, there was a substantial dining area and a ballroom as well as the usual complement of kitchens and offices.

On the first floor were spacious reception rooms and bedrooms and in the grounds lay numerous detached buildings or chalets providing additional guest accommodation. There was, I recall, a singular lack of bedlinen but apart from that no soldier could have asked for a more congenial billet, surrounded by well-kept gardens and within walking distance of the town centre. There was also room in the grounds for our guns and vehicles, and even a garage for my Opel. The officers occupied the main hotel bedrooms, with a mess upstairs, and the other ranks were allotted the chalets, two or three men in each. When we found that most of the pre-war staff of the hotel were out of work and anxious to have their jobs back, we were doing no more than carrying out orders when we took them onto the payroll.

Each battery had a cook seconded from the Army Catering Corps, in our case one Corporal Jenkins, an amiable man from Torquay whose culinary skills were not however great. The impetus to improve our cuisine came from a large Cockney, Gunner Sharp. As one of the many duties foisted on me, while my brother officers were more usefully employed or on their way home, was that of catering officer, Sharp and I got to know each other very well. The rations with which we were issued were well-balanced and adequate, but boring. Even on the beach at Morib we were eating tinned pineapple rings from California when newly picked fresh pineapples were readily available. Gunner Sharp was not happy, for example, to serve reconstituted potatoes or tinned carrots when fresh vegetables were on the market stalls in profusion. Along with the other hotel staff, we had engaged the chefs, who also wanted local fresh ingredients rather than the soya links, meat and vegetable stews, corned beef, Spam, and tinned fish with which we were regularly supplied. The tinned fish was a particular problem.

The inhabitants of Ipoh were not addicted to corned beef or Spam, but they were very keen on tinned fish, and especially the variety with which the Americans generously supplied us. With my knowledge and approval Gunner Sharp set up a trading arrangement with a Chinese woman whereby chicken, fresh vegetables, and other supplies requested by him, Corporal Jenkins, and our Chinese chefs were regularly exchanged for cases of tinned fish. The result was that the quality of food served to the men improved greatly, but not as much as that in the officers' mess, where David Scott, the magistrate, still presided in his military role as battery commander. I cannot recall anyone drawing attention to my success as catering officer, but the customary complaints about army food were, for three or four contented weeks, stilled.

The deal came unstuck because, instead of discreetly introducing the army rations into restaurants, the woman chose to display them on a market stall. The police, newly appointed and keen, would have been blind not to see the markings on the cases, if not on the individual tins, and she found herself charged with stealing the fish. The first I heard about it was when David casually remarked that the matter was coming up for hearing before him the following week. Gunner Sharp had cut off her supplies as soon as the police moved in and, possibly in an attempt to protect my back, he had chosen not to tell me what was afoot. I still believe that David knew more than he let on but Sharp and I, and even Corporal Jenkins, were in an awkward fix. What we had done was not illegal under civil law, but there was certainly something in *King's Regulations* against it. As for the Chinese woman, all she had to do was to tell all, and we would have had no option but to corroborate her story. My dilemma was whether I should come clean to David before the hearing, which might make things difficult for him too, or just allow events to take their course. Clearly, if she were convicted unfairly, we would all have to speak out and face the consequences.

The case came to court while Gunner Sharp and I were still dithering about what we should do. The woman pleaded guilty, and, by way of punishment, David decreed that the fish should be returned to the army. He may have also imposed a small fine. She said nothing in mitigation, nor was anything said on her behalf, and the Court seems not to have been disposed to ask any searching questions about where she obtained the stolen goods. What arrangement she had with Gunner Sharp I never discovered. All I know is that, just before he was repatriated, he assured me that he had seen to it that she had not suffered any loss. The only people who did suffer were the members of 382 Battery, who went back to a diet of reconstituted potatoes, tinned carrots, soya links, meat and vegetable stews, Spam, and American tinned fish. David Scott came out of it best, because he was within days appointed commanding officer, promoted to the rank of lieutenant-colonel, and moved from the Majestic Hotel to the regimental officer's mess where I am sure a more palatable cuisine was available.

I seem to recall that John Adams had left for London to take his Bar examinations before I left Ipoh in August 1945. Gordon Samuels was long gone, and David Scott had followed soon after. In their stead, let us hope, those coming before the courts were being judged by people who spoke their language and were more familiar with their laws and customs than two British army officers from the Royal Devon Yeomanry, one a law student and the other a country solicitor from Kingsbridge.

8

Our Highland Fling

While my battery had been stationed in Bidor in September 1945, it had fallen to a sister unit, 381 Battery, and specifically to 'A' Troop under Glyn Gabe, to take the high road from Tapah into the Cameron Highlands to eject the Japanese and any other malefactors. For people living in modern-day Malaysia, this area, remote and thousands of feet above the plains, is both a holiday resort and a district for the cultivation of temperate crops. For us Caucasians, suffering from prickly heat and having a skin pigmentation unsuited to the tropical sun, it was much more than that: to enjoy the climate of the Highlands was almost like going home. Almost. The big difference, for modest heterosexual young men such as we professed to be, would normally have been the absence of any congenial female company.

The Highlands had provided ideal guerrilla territory during the Japanese occupation, having poor vehicular access and being surrounded by thick jungle. Although the area had no strategic significance, the Japanese must have held it in considerable force. A Japanese colonel formally surrendered to Captain Gabe and handed over his ceremonial sword, as did his fellow officers. A convent, from which the nuns had been evicted early in 1942, had been used by the occupiers as a hospital and also, it would seem from the presence of six young Japanese females resident there, for other non-medical purposes. The colonel insisted the girls were only present because they were suffering from pulmonary tuberculosis, but our regimental medical officer, Tegwyn Jones, was able to refute that dire diagnosis and confirm Glyn's suspicions that their main role had been as 'comfort women'. They, and the rest of the prisoners, were sent down to Tapah for repatriation, each being first relieved of all their belongings apart from a change of clothing, a watch, and a fountain pen. By the time they arrived in Kuala Lumpur, they only had the change of clothing. I do not know what happened to the women.

A handful of Japanese soldiers, unsure no doubt of what to make of the emperor's opaque language, had refused to surrender and had taken to the jungle. The Sakai, the local aboriginal tribe, knew where they were hiding, and led our search party to them. As the wretched men had been subsisting on a diet of nettles, they were probably glad to have been found and bemused when they were given a square meal, medically examined, generally treated as human beings, and sent home.

Glyn did not enjoy the advantage of having a skilled interpreter as I did in Bidor. He communicated with the Japanese colonel through a Malay boy who spoke a little of both their respective languages, augmented by frequent references to a Japanese/English dictionary. There was understandable confusion when the colonel presented Glyn with a box, saying, 'Sackcloth for you'. Its contents turned out not to be something to be worn with ashes as an act of contrition but a finely tailored, light, worsted, grey suit. Glyn was delighted with the gift, specially as it was a good fit, and unwisely showed it to his battery commander, Humphrey Smith. Major Smith thereupon appropriated it for himself. Before the Japanese left the Highlands, the boy disappeared. The colonel told Glyn that he had died and been cremated and although Glyn suspected some kind of foul play, he had no evidence, nor the resources or time in which to inquire further. It may well have been that the lad knew too much to be left alive, and the Japanese wanted him out of the way with war crimes trials pending.

The Smokehouse Inn was a long and low building overlooking the golf course. Despite its long verandah and wooden steps, it followed more closely the architectural style of the Kingston bypass than traditional Malay construction. In January 1942, the staff had buried the equipment to prevent its use by the Japanese, digging it up again when Glyn Gabe arrived with 'A' Troop. When we arrived, the bedrooms were occupied by young nurses and servicewomen who had been sent from Singapore to recover at the high altitude from various dermatological problems. The restaurant was not open to non-residents and the bar much less well-stocked than our own messes. When we went there of an evening, we would hand over a supply of gin, whisky, and rum for consumption by ourselves, our gunners, and our female companions. The only contribution I can recall the Smokehouse making to the quenching of our thirst was when the barman produced some Danish beer.

We drank it, despite its doubtful provenance, and were very unwell later that night.

I was not aware who was managing the Inn during our six weeks in the Highlands. All I can recall is the friendly attention with which we were looked after by the staff, all of whom had been there before the war. Once a week they arranged a dance, with 'Swinging on a Star' and 'Don't Fence Me In' taking the place of the pre-war tunes played in the Ipoh dance halls. The very mention of the Andrews Sisters today evokes a number of youthful memories.

The men of 'A' Troop had been unable to enjoy its delights for very long. After shipping out the last of the Japanese, they were ordered back to the plains, where Glyn himself was seconded to civil duties, and their place was taken by 'F' Troop under John Jones and then Frank Ellen. Frank was in charge when the MPAJA decided to call a strike and contrived to assemble a mob of dissidents who seemed ready to make trouble. He decided the best way to handle the problem was to invite a delegation to his officers' quarters. This was led by a woman short in stature but of ample girth, whose demeanour changed when she saw salacious pin-ups on the walls of the officers' mess, those depicted being less covered with flesh and dress than she was. If she was afraid that such a display might inspire an attack on her own virtue, Frank assures me that she need not have worried. The strike soon fizzled out and apparent peace reigned again.

It would seem that, between the withdrawal of 'F' Troop and our arrival with 'D' Troop (to which I had been transferred because it was down to a single officer), the British garrison in the Highlands had in effect been withdrawn, even though the authorities knew that the local communists from the MPAJA were stirring up trouble. The army was however short of men and the regiment in particular was being constantly denuded by repatriation of its soldiers and by being asked to assume more and more civilian duties. We in 'D' Troop certainly found nobody waiting to hand over to us when we arrived under our troop commander, Neil McGill, a Scottish schoolmaster from the isle of Islay, who had until then been busy, along with Geoff Stavert, in getting the local education system back to normal. When the regiment had its full complement of officers, my move would have been noted in orders and my position as gun position officer made official. Such formalities were no longer being observed.

In accordance with the finest military tradition, Neil told me to find a billet for the troops while he sorted out something comfortable for ourselves. He chose well. Our home for six weeks was a luxurious bungalow on the knoll to the left as you enter the Highlands. It came with a cook and another servant. For the first time in years we found ourselves sleeping on a soft bed between sheets, with a cosy fire in the grate in the evenings. On an occasional table lay magazines from December 1941 and January 1942, abandoned there as the owners had fled. The cupboards were full of clothes, the furniture all in place, and the kitchen well equipped. Nothing had been touched or stolen in the intervening three years, nor had the Japanese moved in. How the normally observant Glyn, John, and Frank had missed such delectable quarters puzzles me to this day. Entering the bungalow, it was as though time had stood still.

We were operating under the usual broad instructions, which included getting the economy going by providing employment and putting money into circulation. My favourite venture was the rehabilitation of the golf course, an amenity which would be important when tourism resumed and one which required my personal daily inspection and trial with the set of clubs I had acquired somewhere along the line. No less than seven holes were playable by the time we were summoned back to Ipoh and the whole course was much improved, although the same could not be said about my golf. More significantly we were ordered to check any attempt by the communists to cause mischief, a task made almost impossible by our lack of an interpreter. The MPAJA men had erected a triumphal arch over the main road as we came over the brow of the hill, surmounted by a Communist red star, and it was not difficult to contrive that one of our lorries collided with it, bringing it down. We were more concerned late one evening when the electric supply failed. Neil suggested rather casually that I should drive down to the generating station to find out what was happening. Fortunately, I had taken my revolver with

Entering Kuala Lumpur in 1945.

The author in Kuala Lumpur, 1946.

Grieg Barr, commanding officer of the Royal Devon Yeomanry, in Ipoh, 1945.

Left to right: Two troop commanders, Glyn Gabe and Gordon Samuels.

Desmond Mangham, who succeeded Bill Noon as assistant adjutant.

Left to right: Jim Guest, Frank Ellen, and Mike Gover.

The first post-war race meeting in Ipoh, Boxing Day, 1945.

The Opel.

me because I found the communist, who had forced the technicians to shut down the station, also to be armed. I would have been better placed however if my weapon had been loaded. I don't know whether the communist spoke English but he understood what I meant when I waved the revolver at him and he left without causing further trouble, although I had to let him keep his gun. I should have collected someone to go with me rather than have driven myself direct from our bungalow, but the men lived in separate quarters some distance away and I hadn't anticipated any trouble. At least the power supply was not again interrupted during our stay but a subsequent search for the armed communist proved fruitless.

We had become reluctant to leave loaded revolvers lying about after an incident at Puttur in India. It was an area of great poverty and our cookhouse was constantly besieged by vagrants. Gunner Brimmacombe, the batman to my then troop commander, Tony Fletcher, decided to frighten them away by brandishing Tony's revolver at them. He was unaware that Tony kept the weapon loaded so that he could fire at tree rats while he rested on his *charpoy* in his *basha*. It is debatable whether Brimmy or the beggars received a greater shock when the weapon went off. Happily nobody was hurt and the venue became less popular with the hungry from then on. Greig Barr, who was then battery commander, told us to leave our revolvers unloaded until we needed to use them in earnest.

We were also charged with picking up some stragglers who

were rumoured to be in the jungle nearby. The locals told us specifically that there were some Jiffs in the area, although I didn't believe it. The Jiffs, or Japanese/Indian Freedom Fighters, included both prisoners-of-war captured and then interned by the Japanese, and men recruited locally. The local volunteers were especially anxious about how we and the people of Malaya would treat them. Neil thought that I should go and have a look. This involved an interesting, but probably unwise, trip into the interior. I used it as an opportunity to try to discover what had happened to a British anthropologist called Noon, who had taken to the jungle in 1942 but had disappeared during the war. A Dutch planter lived locally and he provided a Chinese guide who in turn persuaded a Sakai tribesman to show the two of us the way. The Dutchman had managed to escape internment during the war because he was married to a Japanese woman, although he had undergone some worrying moments and only contrived to retain his freedom by keeping his head well below the parapet. As the Sakai tribe had worked closely with the MPAJA during the occupation and still thought that the communists were the masters, it is easy to conclude with hindsight that our little expedition was ill-conceived.

We had been going about two hours, passing tribesmen with blowpipes and climbing steadily through the jungle, when the Sakai who had been leading the way vanished. The Chinese guide told the Dutchman who told me that the Sakai had seen some birds flying in a certain pattern, which was a bad omen, and we should turn back. I was unhappy merely to retrace our steps because, if someone did want to ambush us, we would have walked into the trap. The Chinese guide said he knew no other way back. We were however beside a stream, which had to run down into the Highlands at some point and, like all soldiers with jungle training, I carried a compass. I suggested to the Dutchman that we cross the stream and find our own way out, which was what we did. Our guide was not keen on coming with us, but we were equally determined that he should not leave us until we were literally out of the woods. It ended in anti-climax. We soon found an easy path down to the valley and arrived back in the Highlands in good order. Nothing more was said about tracing renegade Jiffs or lost anthropologists.

The single track road up the hill from Tapah to the Cameron Highlands was dangerous even without having a large cat jump out at your open jeep from the overhanging bank, as happened the night we returned from the races in Ipoh. Glyn Gabe had been less exposed to danger in his travels on this road, suffering no more than having to follow a lorry laden with smelly durian fruit for several miles. To regulate the traffic, Neil placed a guard on permanent duty at the bottom of the hill, and another at the top, both with field telephones. This gave something for our gunners to do, and provided warning of any unexpected visitor, who would certainly not take the jungle paths to the Highlands which the dastardly Japanese had used for their attack in 1942. Thus the one visit we had from a senior officer during our tour-of-duty was met by an extremely smart turn out by our men. We did not feel obliged to tell him that this was the only formal parade we held while we were up there.

As I have mentioned, the skin of northern Europeans is not well suited to life in the tropics, but a spell at high altitude even near the equator can cure many skin complaints as well as other medical conditions. In India, where we did intensive jungle training before embarking for Malaya, I developed deep ulcers on my ankles which would not respond to medication and only healed when I was sent for a spell into the Nilgiri Hills, accompanied by Philip Shimwell, who had contracted some foul stomach upset. I was cured, although I still carry the scars, but unhappily he wasn't. It was therefore to be expected that the Cameron Highlands should be used as a leave centre for patients suffering mainly from dermatological problems, and this started just before we arrived there. What we did not expect was that almost all the patients would be female, mainly Wrens and nurses from Singapore.

British soldiers on active service in the 14th Army saw very few Western women, and the few they did see did not normally notice any male below the rank of major. Soldiers who sought female company were only likely to find it with local girls. One of our constant concerns was to avoid casualties from venereal disease, such as was contracted by my driver, a Geordie of nineteen, through one unguarded contact when we were in Bidor. A cartoon in our forces' newspaper, SEAC, showing an ugly Wren saying, 'I never knew I was so attractive until I served in the Far East', struck a familiar chord with all of us. (SEAC was reputed to be the best forces newspaper of the war. It was produced by Frank Owen, who had been editor of the London Evening Standard, and therefore in a reserved occupation and not liable for military service. Owen wrote an article which annoyed Ernie Bevin, the Minister of Labour. Bevin sent for his secretary, Harold Rossetti, whom I knew in later years, and asked why Owen was not in the forces. Harold explained that, as an editor, he was exempt. 'I don't care,' replied Bevin, 'call him up.' Within two weeks, the editor had become Private Owen. When Owen arrived in Bombay, Mountbatten was looking for an editor for SEAC and for once the army put the right man in the right job.)

The presence in the Highlands of the Wrens was, for soldiers who had been in the Far East a long time, the icing on the cake. As for the girls, their stay would have been less interesting were it not for the men providing transport for sightseeing. Certainly the dances at the Smokehouse Inn became better attended and less alcoholic through their presence. Neil and I must have neglected our duties by both being away at the same time when we took a weekend trip to Penang with two of the Wrens, an event about which my memories are hazy, apart from recalling the phosphorescence of the sea when we swam late one night from a deserted beach. Our other outing from the Highlands was the trip to Ipoh for the races. As I mentioned previously, my brother, who had obtained a compassionate posting to Kuala Lumpur from Rangoon so that we could be stationed near each other, was spending a week's leave with us at the time, with the result that there was only room in the jeep for one of the girls.

The patients stayed in the Highlands for a week or a fortnight, depending on their medical condition, which was for most of them prickly heat caused by wearing tight clothing. I got to know some of the Wrens who were working on Mountbatten's staff in Singapore, one of whom was a cipher clerk and full of interesting tales about the British royal family with their frequent messages to and from 'Dickie'. I learnt from them more about the political situation than would normally be vouchsafed to a junior officer, and especially what was happening in Sumatra and Java, which made me even more keen to stay in Malaya with the regiment. When they left they urged me to take some time off so that they could show me Singapore. The fact that Singapore was out of bounds for leave did not seem to them an obstacle, nor indeed was it, or not much, as I will recount in a later chapter.

There was another doughty Englishwoman living in the Highlands whom I did not meet, and of whose existence I was unaware until Greig told me about her fifty-nine years later. On release from internment in Changi jail, she had refused to be repatriated, taking the train to Tapah Road, where she asked the subaltern stationed there when the bus left for the Highlands where she had a house. Told there was no bus, she demanded an explanation for the regiment's failure in the two weeks since its arrival to organize public transport. The bemused lieutenant passed her on to regimental headquarters where Greig fed her, found her a bed, and sent her by jeep up the hill the next day. At dinner he asked her if it had been dreadful in Changi. 'It was indeed,' she replied. 'The first night I was there I was put in the same room as a coolie woman. The Japs never made that mistake again.' By such *memsahib*s was the British Empire won, and lost.

All good things come to an end and it was a sad day when we left the Highlands for the last time on being recalled to Ipoh. As Neil was troop commander, it was not appropriate for me to submit a report, although there was plenty to write about with growing evidence of communist influence in the area. Some time later, among our replacement officers there appeared a pleasant but rather inexperienced lieutenant, Freddie B., who was worried that the regiment might not keep him, that he would be posted to Java and become involved in the fighting there. None of us had bothered much about being sent into action while the war was on, but to have to go and risk your neck when it was over was akin to seeing victory snatched from you by a goal scored in injury time. I suggested Freddie might win some favour if he went up to the Highlands and reported on the security situation there. Obviously he couldn't learn much in a short visit and when he came back I drafted the report for him. In the event, it didn't result in his getting any credit for it, although he managed to avoid being sent to Java. When I next saw David Scott, then our commanding officer, he congratulated me on Freddie's report. At least I finally knew that somebody actually read them. Whether they took any notice was a different matter.

And a reminder of the importance of carrying compasses in the jungle: another pertinent SEAC cartoon showed two soldiers in the midst of nowhere. One says, 'I joined the 14th Army to forget.' 'Have you forgotten?' asks the other. 'Yes, I've forgotten my compass.'

9

Going Downhill

When we first visited Ipoh on our evenings out in September 1945, cigarettes were the preferred currency, with a circular tin of fifty Players or Gold Flake being the equivalent of a high denomination note. It was through this medium of exchange that I acquired a number of British colonial stamps hand-blocked in red and black through overprinting by the Japanese, which I was able to add to the collection I had liberated in Bidor. In the weeks during which we had been stationed in Ipoh, prior to being sent up to the Cameron Highlands, the community's return to normality had been too gradual to be noticeable. Coming down the hill again after six weeks away was to discover another world. Streets which had carried only army vehicles and cycles were now busy with civilian cars and lorries. On the pavements you could see faces of Europeans who were not wearing jungle green, and locally recruited policemen in uniform. The two Western-style cinemas were showing recently released Hollywood films. Bookshops stocked current magazines from England. Everywhere people seemed busy and there was plenty of food and clothing in the shops. In the Jubilee and Celestial dancehalls the melodies of 1941 had been replaced by those popularized in the intervening years through the renditions of Betty Grable, Rita Hayworth, June Allyson, Bing Crosby, Vera Lynn, Perry Como, and other virtuosi.

I never saw any announcement that the British Military Administration had come to an end, although the number of officials in newly opened offices in the town confirmed that our brief moment of power was over. Instead of patrolling the plantations and villages as my battery had been doing, we were now ordered to mount guard by night over places which did not appear to be under any imminent threat of enemy assault or to contain anything liable to be stolen. By day, formal parades had started and, as I seemed to spend much of my time as orderly officer along with other mundane duties, I decided that it was better to lay up half the vehicles, permanently prepared for inspection by being kept glossy with a mixture of oil and petrol, and to hide the other half out of the way while they accumulated dirt through running on the road and very occasionally doing something useful.

Greig Barr had long since left for home, and been succeeded as commanding officer first by David Scott, and then, briefly, by Robert Hudson, before a regular soldier who had served in Northern Europe came to take over. Of the nine officers who had been with our battery when we left India in 1945, by May 1946 only two of us remained, the others having been moved to other jobs for a few brief weeks before they too departed. My fellow survivor, Michael Shorter, had been in danger of being left behind in India because the regiment was over-strength when it embarked for Malaya and, as he had for several months been trying to teach himself to play the clarinet, with constant practice but no discernible improvement, there were some among us who, solely on that score, would not have been too upset to have left him behind. In the event and after representations had been made, another, less congenial, subaltern drew the short straw and Michael stayed with the regiment. He was a charming companion but perhaps more intellectual and less adventurous or irresponsible than some of us. He put me off clarinets for life.

Changes of a similar nature had also taken place among the ranks of the non-commissioned officers and gunners. Of the four sergeants in my old troop, three including Sergeant Peasey had gone home, two with their time up and one on compassionate release after learning that his wife, and mother of his two young children, was pregnant by an American soldier. The daddy of us all, Battery Sergeant Major Truscott, an engine driver from Totnes in Devon, had left us in India when a three-day exercise in Cocanada had weeded out most of the older men as not being fit enough for jungle warfare, including our commanding officer and the second-in-command. 'Old Trussy' had known most of the Territorial volunteers who originally made up the battery personally, many of them recruited in his hometown, and in some cases he also knew their families. With his departure and that of the sergeants, the battery had lost that bit more of its cohesion and its spirit.

My troop commander in the Highlands, Neil McGill, was promoted and moved to other duties as soon as we arrived back in Ipoh. The traditional organization of the battery into a headquarters and two troops seemed to have become a thing of the past. I think my title had become command post officer, the person who has the responsibility at battery headquarters for seeing that the guns all point in the right direction when you go into action, and especially that you don't shell your own people. In practice it didn't matter what I was called as we were doing no artillery training and our main concern was to prevent our fellow gunners, and ourselves, from getting into trouble out of boredom.

The regiment was at this time seriously under strength. Its role as a service unit had suffered because, apart from the one fortuitous round at Taiping, we had done no firing of live ammunition since we landed in Malaya. With so many officers seconded to civilian duties, along with other experienced men, there had been nobody to organize practice exercises. Routine gun drill, where you go through the motions on the parade ground, was also neglected. Demobilization of the longest serving people had started before we left India. Many of those who left then had been pre-war Territorials and had served for six years. After November 1945, when demobilization resumed, every two weeks or so, numbers of senior soldiers were on their way to Singapore and the boat home as 'their number came up'. We were also losing men for posting to other units, although, as already noted, this was usually an excuse to get rid of the less satisfactory or more troublesome elements.

The relatively few gunners who joined us were for the most part young men who had been called up within the last year. Having been conscripted when the war in Europe was over, few welcomed having been shipped halfway round the world to while away their time in a theatre where the other war had now ended. We also received new officers, most of whom had not been previously in a service unit but had been engaged in transit camps, railway stations, arms dumps, and similar necessary but unexacting duties, which seemed to have commanded a higher rank than they would have achieved in a regiment. When they came to us, especially when they were not reduced in rank, it was difficult to fit them in, and impracticable to assign to them duties consistent with their seniority. In my battery, and probably in the other two also, the battery commander resolved the dilemma by putting most of the duties on the subalterns who had been with the regiment since it left England. We at least had the advantage of knowing the men, and they us.

The loss of old comrades and the lack of interest on the part of those who came to replace them were not good for morale. I suppose we should have been more tolerant of the new arrivals and tried harder to make them feel at home, but the few surviving members of the old guard, which included me, regretted the loss of comradeship and shared experiences which had made serving in the regiment a stimulating existence, and most of us were not thoughtful or mature enough to make much of an effort to forge a similar relationship with our new colleagues. I recall an incident one evening when Nehru, the nationalist leader who was to become President of India, had come to Ipoh to make a speech on the *padang*. Not unnaturally I wanted to see and hear the great man, but none of the newcomers was prepared to come with me. I assured them that we would not be attacked and this was an opportunity not to be missed. So I went on my own. I received a few ritual scowls from my neighbours and was disappointed at being too far away to hear clearly what he was saying, even though he spoke in English.

There were other unwelcome changes under the new regime. We were expected to dress up and attend dinner in the officers' mess every evening, after an hour or so drinking in the ante-room, and not to leave the table until the mess president, the senior officer present, decided he wanted to go. We were discouraged from going out on the town and from mixing with our men in the dancehalls or the Happy World amusement park. We could no longer draw weapons and ammunition for a patrol without signing for them, and then accounting for any rounds we used, which had the result that often we didn't bother to arm ourselves as before because of the paperwork involved. Firing a weapon became taboo. With regard to censorship, I was reminded, without being reprimanded, that I must actually read the men's letters home—eight months after the war had ended—and not just seal them without looking at them. (My not doing this previously may help explain why the post had been unusually heavy when I was acting as orderly officer.) There were renewed, but now plausible, threats of action against any officer who, as in the past, used a jeep as his personal transport. And so on. If this was peacetime soldiering, I preferred what had gone before.

The authorities seemed to have become paranoid about the use of jeeps by officers. Until then we nearly always drove ourselves on official business. When Philip Shimwell was on his way home, he declined to take the train from Ipoh to Singapore, only to be hounded after arriving back in England for the value of some tools which had supposedly been stolen from the jeep which took him to the boat. For someone who had fought in Normandy and served with distinction for five or six years, this was, to say the least, an ungenerous parting gesture on the part of the War Office.

I have mentioned our medical officer, Tegwyn Jones, in the context of the Japanese 'comfort women' in the Cameron Highlands. The regiment also hosted an officer seconded from the Royal Corps of Signals, Robert Steven, and, for a brief period, a padre, although I cannot recall ever attending any church services. Each of these officers was provided with his own jeep and was allowed to drive himself. The padre, a Scottish Presbyterian minister, was unfortunate enough to contract a complaint which required his going to hospital in Kuala Lumpur. A malicious rumour was put about that the disease with which he was afflicted was not one from which you would expect a man of the cloth to suffer. Tegwyn declined, on the grounds of medical etiquette, to confirm or deny it, when I tackled him about it. The padre not only took with him his jeep to Kuala Lumpur but made no arrangements for its return to the regiment. Reg Ferguson, then our adjutant, thoughtfully suggested that I might like to go to recover the jeep, and at the same time spend a day or two with my brother. However, my battery-commander-of-the-month (we had five different commanders of 382 Battery in a space of six months) felt I had been too often away from his benevolent gaze and someone else made the trip. Another scurrilous report alleged that the padre had actually been seen in a ward dedicated to patients suffering from a venereal disease. If so, I am sure it must have been that he was ministering to the unfortunate victims. We never saw him again and the short-lived attempt to save our souls was not repeated, leaving us to resume our progress along the many roads to perdition which we chose to take. This refusal to allow us to use military transport affected me less than most, partly because I had the Opel and partly because I chose to ignore it.

Another unwelcome feature of that time was the arrival in the town of various officers from non-service units, most of them captains or above, who seemed to have no obvious reason for being there. Although none of them had any dealings with the regiment, we saw them as interlopers in 'our' Ipoh. Their number was reduced fortuitously when one of them, apparently crossed in love, got out of bed, shaved, and then shot himself in the head. His interment was the same day in the early afternoon and I was sent to be a pallbearer, even though I had never met the unfortunate chap. As I watched the funeral service from the front pew, I noticed blood dripping from the makeshift coffin. Obviously someone had been a little too profligate with the formalin or parsimonious with the plywood. I then saw that my shoulder, where I had rested the coffin, was also covered in blood. I was very quick off the mark, when the service ended, to take the end where his feet were.

The battery still occupied the Majestic Hotel but, with its shortage of officers and consequent spare accommodation, our mess became the involuntary host to many transient officers looking for a meal and a bed for the night, as well as for others stationed in Ipoh for whatever reason who had nowhere else to lay their heads. Prominent among our uninvited guests were Dutch officers who had arrived from Europe with the intention of restoring their control over Indonesia. It is difficult to deal with this episode on the basis of what we knew then rather than what I have read since, just as I have not always found it easy to explain my suspicions and feelings in those days about the guerrillas in the MPAJA and the communists, knowing what transpired later. My information about Java in particular had been gleaned mostly from Mountbatten's Wrens in the Cameron Highlands, to the effect that things were far from being under control, that we had had to rearm some Japanese troops to help fight against the nationalists, and that, to put it mildly, the Dutch were not receiving the kind of passive welcome in Java and

Sumatra that we had experienced in Malaya.

Before leaving England, I had received an insight into the mind-set of a minority of the inhabitants of the Low Countries under the German occupation, which differed from the propaganda being put out in Britain by the Ministry of Information. When I was at the OCTU at Catterick in Yorkshire in the spring of 1944, three young Belgians arrived to join the squad. They kept pretty well to themselves and I did not get to know them until two of them and I were summoned back to camp from the Lake District halfway through Battle School (where it was mandatory that every cadet completed the full course before he could be commissioned). We took the circuitous train journey from Carlisle to Newcastle to Darlington to Richmond together, wondering which of our misdemeanours had come to light so serious as to justify our urgent recall. On the journey they told me how two of them had made their way through German-occupied France to Spain, where they had been interned, so that they could enlist. They were unwilling to reveal how the third cadet had escaped. I was hugely impressed to learn of their courage and resourcefulness, but also surprised to hear their stories of collaboration with the Germans by some elements in the Low Countries, and of less than universal support in Holland in particular for the Allied cause.

They had left Belgium a few months before the landings took place in Normandy, when it was not yet clear to those in occupied Europe that Germany would lose the war. We now know that under difficult and dangerous circumstances most Dutch people not unnaturally kept their heads down during the German occupation, and that around one per cent of the Dutch population was active in resisting the occupiers prior to the courageous strike by railway workers in 1944. This led to the Germans cutting off food supplies and thus to mass starvation among those Dutch people whose territory had not been freed by the Allied advance.

I had expected the Dutch officers who came to Ipoh to have the same concept of freedom, as an entitlement of everyone and not subject to selectivity, which had characterized my Belgian friends. Some of them may have done, but others were only interested in subjugating the inhabitants of Sumatra and Java to renewed rule from Holland by whatever means came to hand. Most of us had picked up a weapon such as a Luger pistol as a souvenir. In addition to my sporting rifle, I had a nickel-plated revolver which looked like a toy but was a real gun, firing .2 bullets. The Dutch were anxious to obtain these personal weapons, so much so that a major, negotiating in the mess for a Tommy gun, pulled the trigger and sprayed the room with bullets. Luckily it was not pointing in my direction. While all of us wanted to see an end to the fighting in Indonesia, I don't think there were many who were anxious to take an active part in helping to reinstate Dutch colonial rule, any more than we wanted to be involved in imposing any political settlement on Malaya against the wishes of the population, or denying India her freedom. We were surprised that our views on colonialism were not always shared by our guests. For that and other reasons I refused to part with my revolver.

Apart from failing to shoot me, the Dutch nearly landed me in real trouble. To keep my gunners out of mischief, I ran a series of unofficial driving courses and competitions on the Ipoh airfield, where the only sign of aviation was a row of abandoned Zero fighter planes but the runway remained in good order. These courses were very popular because in those days few young men had had the chance of learning to drive in civilian life. Arriving early one morning to take a class, I was aghast to see a tracked Bren gun carrier racing up and down the runway, tearing up the surface in the process. I pulled my jeep ahead of it to stop it, and had the back of the vehicle, including the carrier for the jerry-can, torn off by one of the tracks. The Dutch colonel driving the vehicle was less than gracious when I ordered him to leave. Fortunately my artificer friend, ASM Major, covered up the jeep's absence for a week while he had it repaired by the REME depot. It had been a close call, because I had been guilty of various infringements of regulations, including driving the jeep myself. The incident did nothing to endear me to our Dutch guests.

If I had thought more carefully, I would not have been so impatient about the regiment's changed role after May 1945.

We, and no doubt other service units in Singapore and the peninsula, had for seven or eight months provided the country with the *best* form of government, one in which there were no politicians or bureaucrats, where those in power had no interest in perpetuating their rule or profiting personally, and where authority confined itself to providing the conditions under which individual citizens could lead peaceful lives and generate wealth. We provided security against the communists, stopped any looting, and prevented smuggling; we did what was

necessary to make public transport available; we helped repair utilities providing water, electricity, and drainage; we organized repair works on the roads and bridges; we put a new currency into circulation and assisted in re-establishing normal banking and credit for businesses; we found work for employees on the plantations and elsewhere until regular conditions returned; we aided local teachers in normalizing education; we supplied impartial magistrates for the courts; and we performed other similar functions which are the duty of any enlightened government. Beyond that, unlike other people who assume power, we did not interfere. The recovery of the economy and the rapid return to normal life was due entirely to the intelligence, initiative, and hard work of the people of Singapore and Malaya. We provided the referee and linesmen, but it was their pitch on which they played the game and won the match.

And our summons from Battle School to Catterick? There was a hockey match between the Gunner OCTU and the Signals OCTU and we three had been recalled to play in the team. We won 2–0. The three of us were commissioned without passing Battle School.

10

Fun, Games, and Salvation

Before we were stationed in Ipoh, we often visited the town in the evening using the Opel. Even in the early days and weeks, there was a lot more going on there than in downtown Bidor, which I recall was little more than a few shops fronting a dusty street. My fellow officers had been able to steal a march on me in their pursuit of pleasure because of my involvement in stripping the Japanese soldiers of their loot. However I soon caught them up, not having missed much because, until the new currency became available, there was a limit to what could be bought. My only handicap was that I seemed to be in excessive demand as orderly officer, an arduous role which included staying in the camp, inspecting the guard, sipping whisky, and playing cribbage with the battery commander. However the Opel was *my* car, and, whatever the demand from my friends, if I was free I was always sure of a seat in it, even if it meant leaving someone else behind.

We usually ended up in one of Ipoh's two dancehalls, where the bands played ballroom dancing tunes which had been in vogue prior to 1942—quicksteps, waltzes, and slow foxtrots—and the taxi-dancers, as in the song, cost ten cents a dance. The girls in the Jubilee Cabaret, which we favoured over the Celestial, were all Chinese, except for a comely Filipina named Gloria, whose mother sat chaperoning her, performing a dual function: anyone who fancied a long-term, or even a short-term, relationship with Gloria would have second thoughts on seeing her mother. I cannot express a view on whether any of the girls were prepared to indulge in extra-curricular activities. I can confirm however that they were, as you might expect, very good dancers and one of them in particular was determined to improve my terpsichorean skills, if only to protect her toes and shins. As she also partnered a better performer, our star cricketer and soccer player Lance-Bombardier Hornsby, whose relationship with her seemed to be closer than mine was, the lessons were much interrupted if he was around.

I should explain that those of us who had been in our early teens when the war broke out in 1939 had become skilled in many arcane subjects, but not in ballroom dancing. At the age of fifteen, we had been put into uniform in a Junior Training Corps and taught how to arrange our puttees around our calves, for all the world as if we were going back to the trenches of 1918. By sixteen, when we joined the Home Guard, we had already thrown hand grenades and fired .303 rifles. We then moved on to Bren guns, Sten guns, and more exotic weapons such as the Northover projector, the Molotov cocktail, and the Blacker Bombard and, at eighteen, in the Senior Training Corps, we were playing with converted First World War split-trail 18/25-pounder guns and firing live shells. This military progression made the induction of recruits into the forces at eighteen-and-a-half run smoothly, but our social graces had suffered as a result. In ballroom dancing, most Europeans lead, and are led, from the shoulders. Oriental dancers dance from the hips, something which I failed to appreciate until many years later.

We virtually never ate out, and never went drinking in bars or the club overlooking the *padang*, much used by expatriates, possibly because alcohol was much more plentiful and cheaper in our messes. We took for granted the privilege as officers of honorary membership of expatriate clubs in India and Malaya. In our early days there was nowhere to go anyway, and my twenty-first birthday party is the only occasion I can recall our dining out in Ipoh. Although we had few problems with drunkenness, there was, for two reasons, no shortage of hard liquor. In 1942, a recently called-up accountant in Delhi, given the task of ordering stores for the 14th Army, put his decimal point in the wrong place when he was working out the supply of spirits, with the result that ten times more than the standard ration of whisky, gin, and rum was available. When General Slim was told of the error, he told his Quartermaster General to issue it anyway. The second factor was that in our Indian Division there were a number of units whose men, for religious reasons, did not touch alcohol. Our access to these redundant stores would have been more difficult had not Bill Noon, then our assistant adjutant, been seconded to brigade headquarters in Tapah to deal with rationing and supply. The rum was free but we had to pay $3 (Straits) for a bottle of Canadian Club or Old Smuggler whisky, and $2.50 for a bottle of Canadian gin.

The one place where we had a chance of meeting the local

community on equal terms was on the sports field. We played cricket on the *padang* at Ipoh, under the captaincy of Frank Ellen and thanks to the foresight of Mr Am Eam Hoch, who had hidden the club's cricket gear from the Japanese by burying it. He was the editor of the local paper, and a batsman of considerable skill, being especially strong on the off side. The hockey team, which I captained, also played on the *padang*, and two of us were flattered by being asked to turn out for the Perak side. I didn't play rugby and so I don't know what those who did got up to, except that I saw strong men limping after some brutal encounters with a local side which included a number of burly Sikhs.

I should have been interested in the soccer team because it was a game I enjoyed. As a newly enlisted private, I had played for the depot of the Lincolnshire Regiment, and as a cadet, for the permanent staff of the OCTU (after my troop, selected from only thirty-five men, had humiliated them by winning). But officers weren't meant to play soccer and, although eventually I was allowed to appear for my battery (out of position at left back), I was excluded from the regimental team except as a referee. One of their first matches in Ipoh in December 1945 was against the Ramblers, who were trounced 13–0. The regiment could however only draw with the Selangor Chinese team in Kuala Lumpur in January and was beaten 4–0 by the Dutch in the same month. Their moment of glory arrived in September 1946, when they won the Malaya Command

Competition, beating the 1st Battalion of the Northamptonshire Regiment from Singapore, but by then I had gone home.

Refereeing regimental soccer matches was not always straightforward. While in India at Puttur, the regiment took on the divisional side. The 81st West African Division, to which we were then attached, had fought with great gallantry in the Arakan. Its soldiers had been recruited on the promise they would only spend one year overseas, and their return to Nigeria and the Gold Coast was long overdue. Understandably they were more than a little miffed about this. Before the kick-off the divisional commander sent me a message saying that, if there were not to be a riot, the division must not lose. I contrived to make it a draw, ignoring unkind comments from my colleagues, on and off the field, about incipient myopia.

In Ipoh, we played tennis on the courts on the *padang*, in front of the club, and badminton in the racecourse building. The golf course was laid around the racetrack and required local knowledge if you wished to avoid injury. At the second hole, you drove over the white wooden rails lining the racetrack about twenty yards in front of the tee. If your shot hit the rails, the ball come back at a height and velocity which might well decapitate you. A prudent player therefore chose to drive with a number 3 iron rather than a wood, even though it was a long hole. The seventh hole was troublesome for a different reason. After rain any lofted shot would plug. Even if you managed to find the ball, which was difficult, the lie was impossible.

Too wise to accept any challenges from the local badminton players who were in a different class from us, we allowed ourselves to be entrapped by the Chinese members of the golf club. Having seen them playing, we were confident, when they threw down the gauntlet, that we could beat them. It seemed uncivil not to accept their generous offer of a lunch before the match, or to neglect to down the many toasts which followed the meal. When I reached the first tee, I had a problem deciding which of two or three balls to hit. Judging by their performance, the same double vision was affecting other members of our team. We recovered a bit over the second nine holes, but the damage had been done. Our hosts were reluctant to give us a return match.

From the above account, and previous revelations, you may think that we were leading a comfortable life, but it is a poor soldier who fails to make the best of things. What the British members of the 14th Army, from General Slim down, did not normally get to enjoy was leave. There was something called Python, or home leave, which so far as I could see nobody got. Then there were two other varieties, Leave in Addition to Python and Leave in Lieu of Python, which some people may have got, but I never met anyone who did, nor did I ever find out what was the difference between them. I was therefore taken aback in June 1946, when the colonel summoned me to his office and told me that I had been on duty continuously for far too long and it was time for me to take a week off. My last break had been my spell in the Nilgiri Hills in India, to get rid of leg ulcers. Previous to that, my (embarkation) leave in November 1944 had coincided with a concentrated German air raid on my home town, which resulted in some 45 deaths in a ball-bearing works, and for me (as for all other able-bodied males) a night spent putting out incendiaries. The suet factory was also set ablaze and, as the bombs kept falling, the gutters in the streets ran with burning fat.

My problem was choosing where to go. I had friends in Penang, but didn't fancy spending a full week on the island. I had enjoyed the Cameron Highlands, but again I had passed several weeks there already. Obviously the best thing would be to get in touch with my Wren friends in Singapore. They had invited me down there, and I would be able to call on my brother in Kuala Lumpur on the way down. There were two snags to this plan. The first was that I dared not risk taking the Opel and we were forbidden to use army transport for private purposes. The second was that Singapore was out of bounds for leave.

A week later, my driver, Gunner Tripp, and I left for Singapore by jeep. We stopped in Kuala Lumpur, where I duly visited my brother in his RAF camp and we toured the city together, having our photographs taken to send home. Not having been back to Kuala Lumpur since the previous September, I was astounded at the transformation that had taken place. The streets were busy with vehicles, the shops well stocked, and everyone was bustling around with a purposeful air.

As my brother was unable to find us a bed, we sought out an artillery unit where, to my delight, I discovered John Honour, a good friend who had been in my troop at OCTU. For his part, aside from his expression of pleasure in seeing me again, Captain Honour took unworthy delight in observing that his former senior under-officer was still only a lieutenant. After chewing the fat at length with Honest John (as he was known), Tripp and I resumed our journey south. I should explain, that being appointed senior under-officer at the field gunnery 125 OCTU was not the mark of distinction which you might assume. In the twelfth week, the members of the troop voted by secret ballot to elect one of their number for this post, but their choice could be vetoed by the officer in charge—in this case, David Scott. As a keen and efficient candidate might make life less agreeable for all, we tended to go for someone who was likely to be the least officious, smart, or studious among our fellows, yet remaining acceptable to the powers-that-be. In effect, the election was decided on the basis of the Lowest Common Denominator rather than the Highest Common Factor.

If the change in Kuala Lumpur over nine months was a surprise, the condition of Singapore was a revelation, and a shock. The previous September, after handing over my trainload of Japanese, I had strolled into the Raffles Hotel, joined a merchant navy engineer for breakfast (who incongruously produced a carton of free-flowing salt at the table), and then made my way back to the station. I never thought of paying for my meal and there was no cash currency anyway. The other people in the hotel were skeletal men newly released from Changi jail and waiting for a passage home, their heads skull-like, their movement slow, their wasted limbs like stalks. The streets were idle, with few civilians about and even fewer troops. In the harbour, gangs of Japanese prisoners carried cargo aboard a ship, running up and down the gangplanks, for all the world like columns of ants. The whole city had a hangdog air.

Now, nine months later, Gunner Tripp and I drove up to the Raffles to be confronted by a uniformed doorman and to be told that the hotel was full. In the early afternoon, the lobby was already awash with officers who were all senior to me. The whole city was vibrant, the pavements and streets crowded with traffic and people. British military uniforms were everywhere. After meeting one of my Wren friends, I found it easy enough to secure a bed for Gunner Tripp with an artillery unit, but not for myself. I spent an uncomfortable night in a transit camp, where undue interest was taken about my particulars by a clerk on the gate, and I moved out without breakfast before any more questions could be asked.

Apart from one day, when we took a picnic, drove up towards Mersing on Malaya's south-east coast, and bathed in the South China Sea, the demands of duty in the cipher section at the headquarters of South-East Asia Command meant that going anywhere with a female companion was confined to the afternoons and evenings. That second day, having collected

Gunner Tripp from his billet, he and I repaired to the Salvation Army canteen, where we knew there would be no segregation between officers and other ranks. I asked the lady serving if she had any idea where I could find a bed for a few nights. She turned out to be the wife of the husband-and-wife team running the Salvation Army operation in Singapore and immediately invited me to stay in their flat, which was close by. So it was I found salvation, in that I had somewhere to lay my head, and indeed a plausible answer should questions again be asked as to why I was in Singapore. While I was staying with them, these good people never sought in any way to involve me in the Salvation Army's activities, nor would they accept any payment for themselves.

While I, as an officer, was an honorary member of the Tanglin Club which had already restored its fine social and sporting facilities and was the best private club in Singapore, Tripp, as a gunner, was refused admittance. With the mornings at our disposal, we solved this dilemma by going for a swim at the Lido where there were no such distinctions. At this time, it had become common for thieves to steal jeeps, or their wheels. Some friends who went swimming at night in Penang came off the beach to find their jeep jacked-up on bricks with all the wheels missing, while Glyn Gabe had suffered the embarrassment of a puncture on Boxing Day after his spare wheel had been stolen while he was soberly carrying out his duties the previous evening, or so he contends. Gunner Tripp had fixed our spare in a manner which made its removal too complex an operation for a sneak-thief. As many drivers immobilized their jeeps by removing the rotor arm from the distributor, thieves had taken to carrying spare rotor arms. To counteract this villainy, Tripp had devised a way of immobilizing our jeep while leaving the rotor arm in place. And then, one morning while we were having our leisurely swim, someone stole our rotor arm. We were hardly in a position to go to a maintenance unit and indent for a replacement but my stalwart friend assured me that he would be able to solve the problem, and indeed he did. I did not ask how, nor did I want to know.

There was great excitement among the cipher Wrens when one of their number was married in Singapore's cathedral to a lieutenant commander. Although I remember the ceremony well, I am unable to recall much about the subsequent reception. Laurence Olivier's film *Henry V* was showing in town, and we saw that too. The days passed quickly and for reasons which I cannot precisely recall, Tripp and I left Singapore rather later than planned. We were in consequence unable to pause in Kuala Lumpur to see my brother and Honest John. It was straight back to Ipoh and to what had become a tedious routine.

It is wrong to regret anything. If however I were to allow myself that indulgence, I would confess that I could have done more during that week in Singapore than go swimming, see my friends, and take a couple of trips over the causeway to the mainland. It was not until I returned to England three months later that I realized how quickly and completely Singapore had recovered from the Japanese occupation. It was not just a matter of the absence of damage to buildings. The whole demeanour of the people on the streets was purposeful. They looked well fed, well dressed, and happy. There were no beggars. The city was clean and free of litter. The contrast with my brief visit nine months earlier was stark.

I had, as I mentioned above, acquired presents for my brother and my elder sister through the generosity of the Japanese in Bidor. I needed to find something suitable for my parents, and my younger sister, who was then nine years old and of whom I had seen little since she had been evacuated to Scotland in 1939. My Wren friends were full of ideas, and eventually, after visiting a number of shops, we bought my sister a *cheongsam*, the simple but attractive garment which Chinese women wear. I was not conscious of it being at all remarkable that, within so short a time after the war, shops offered a great variety of choice in clothing, and much else, without any restrictions on purchase. It was only when I returned to dismal and rationed England that I realized what a miracle had been performed by the people in the Far East.

About the only sight-seeing Tripp and I did was to visit Changi Prison, which housed many of the former Japanese jailers. We talked about leaving the city a day or two early on our return so that we could visit Malacca, but decided against it. We were less likely to arouse suspicion from the military police if we kept to the main highway north. Thinking back to those few days in June 1946, I have not been surprised at Singapore's commercial success. I have been back a few times but, with its high-rise buildings, its resemblance now to other great cities, and its traffic, it no longer has the unique charm which I remember from long ago. Bliss was it in that dawn to be young, but to be alive (still) was very heaven!

11

Home Again, Home Again

My last weeks in Malaya were marred by niggling issues, none of which would have caused so much concern if things had remained as they had been under Greig Barr, David Scott, or Robert Hudson. One, relating to a question of discipline, also made some of us wonder how we could be expected to keep up morale; the lack of excitement and long absence from home were bound to cause frustration among our men. If however I was frustrated by what was happening during the summer of 1946, Alan Maidens, who was not released for another nine months, told me that from then on life in the regiment became increasingly more difficult, especially after it had left Ipoh.

By May 1946, the battery had been much changed through demobilization and inward postings. The men, of all ranks, who had arrived in Malaya from India had been together for a long time. In the battery a word from Sergeant Major Truscott had been enough to bring an offender into line, without any formal disciplinary procedures. In those days, I never knew of anyone being put on a charge for misbehaviour. The mere suggestion that a miscreant might be left behind or posted was enough to restore order. It was disappointing then, under the new dispensation, to see a gunner receive the order 'Cap off, belt off', and be marched in before the battery commander to be punished for some trivial offence arising out of his boredom, which could and should have been settled by a quiet word.

One of the many who joined the battery in Ipoh was a young man who was good at football, knew he was good at football, and expected everyone to defer to him because he was good at football. He soon found a place in the regimental team and thought that this distinction placed him above his fellows, and that his military obligations were being fully discharged on the soccer field. Not surprisingly, this attitude did not go down too well with everyone around him, especially as he was a recent arrival. Nor did it go down well with me when he was lazy, sullen, and insolent. In the limbo in which we existed he was a source of friction which we could do without.

Because I had naturally got to know our men better than the transient officers who by now came and went so frequently, one of my jobs was to recommend people for posting-out of the battery to serve in Java which, as I have already indicated, was not the most popular destination for those whose only ambition was to serve their time out quietly and be demobilized in one piece as soon as possible. I normally used the industrial principle of last in, first out. There were however a few instances where the unit would be a happier place if someone left, and I decided that this was one of them. The uproar when I had the audacity to suggest that a talented member of the football team should be posted, and to Java of all places, took me by surprise. I was asked to reconsider the recommendation. I did reconsider it and then confirmed it. Without wanting to sound sanctimonious, I thought it more important that we should retain a disciplined and cohesive unit, despite the pressures of impending demobilization and boredom, rather than that the regiment should perform well on the football field. My battery commander, another in the sequence of those who appeared, stayed awhile, and then moved on in the revolving door syndrome, did not overrule me, but his support was somewhat tepid. In the end, the matter was resolved by the recalcitrant gunner being transferred to another battery, thus staying in the regiment. Possibly I was wrong. Perhaps success at sport as a morale booster was more important than discipline, effectiveness, comradeship, and good manners. But I didn't think so then, nor do I today.

Another tiresome issue arose when I had to answer questions arising from the battery's occupation of the Majestic Hotel, and its retention of the hotel staff. The major investigating the matter, who was based in Singapore, was adamant that he could only deal with an officer in 382 Battery who had also been there when we moved into the hotel. As most of the other officers had departed, that left just Michael Shorter and myself. Michael knew no more about it than I did, but was too nice a person to take a robust line on anything contentious or stand up to bluster. We decided that I had better deal with it. The first thing I was asked to produce was our requisitioning order. What was that? It was explained to me that no army unit was permitted to occupy private premises without such a document.

I told him that we had frequently occupied private premises before we came to Malaya, and since, when it was necessary to carry out our duties, and as far as I was aware nobody had ever issued any paperwork, let alone anything called a requisitioning order, which was something with which I was unfamiliar. If we had failed in our duty in obtaining such an order, he warned me, the responsible officers could be surcharged the cost of occupying the premises. It was all in *King's Regulations*. And what about the staff? What justification did we have for taking on all the hotel personnel, including the cooks and the gardeners? (And the hairdresser, I added, trying to help him get his facts right.) Who was going to refund the salaries we had been paying them all these months? Again, he started talking about surcharges, which would have to be met by all those involved and especially, it would seem, by myself and Michael Shorter.

It was my habit in those days to be civil to those officers who were senior to me, which was almost everyone, but this was an occasion when I nearly broke that rule. Was he not aware that in the autumn of 1945 we had been instructed to give employment to as many people as possible, so as to get the economy moving again? Had he not been told that at the same time we had been ordered to spend as much money as we reasonably could so as to get currency into circulation as quickly as possible? Things may, I suggested, have looked different from SEAC headquarters in Colombo or Kandy, or wherever he was stationed at the time, but the soldiers on the ground in Malaya had not done so bad a job in seeing off the MPAJA, preventing crime, and overseeing the restoration of a normal pattern of life, without the assistance of any civil power. If we had cut a few corners, it was because the corners needed cutting. The discussion came to an abrupt end when he said he was going to report the matter, and me, to my commanding officer. I never saw him, or heard anything about him, again.

A more serious incident followed which convinced me it really was time I went home and indeed it was to precipitate my departure.

Soon after my trip to Singapore, I was detailed to take a squad of men for a week to guard an arms dump situated in some caves a few miles from Ipoh, where the limestone hills drop down into the plain. The geographical formation reminded me, albeit on a smaller scale, of the Cheddar Gorge in the west of England, with high bluffs on either side of a canyon and a number of caves in the cliff faces. The jungle, although thick at the top of the escarpment, was certainly passable on foot. The site was protected at its mouth by a wire fence where a track ran from the main highway but was otherwise open to any intruder approaching on foot from the cliff tops. As usual, we had no rules of engagement. All I was told was that it had been a Japanese arsenal.

Apart from the absence of wire, there were no floodlights or other means of keeping the caves under observation at night. Some of the stores had doors, and some of the doors were locked. Others did not, and were not. I took over the duty from an Indian infantry unit, and when their officer handed me an inventory, I refused to sign it because there was no means of checking it. In fact, I refused to sign anything. We had been issued with rations for the week and my only memory is of doing the rounds one night and, as I drove to an isolated post, seeing a large black cat some seven feet long, prowling around. I decided it would be better not to tell the sentry, Gunner Smith, 'Smudger' as all Smiths were, about his feline companion. At the end of the week, during which I had received no visit or communication from the regiment, I handed over to another detachment of the same Indian unit that we had relieved, and gave their officer the inventory, without asking him to sign it. And that, I thought, was that: except that as usual I wrote a full report to the regiment, detailing the lack of security at the site, the impossibility of guarding it adequately without wire and lights, and the folly of leaving an arms dump in such an accessible place when there was known communist agitation in the region. I suggested that it would be better to have the Royal Engineers destroy the stores rather than leave them there.

In the last week of July, I was summoned to regimental headquarters where I was interviewed by a young officer from the Judge Advocate-General's (JAG's) office in Singapore. He told me that, during our week's duty at the caves, there had been significant thefts by communists from the arsenal, and that I was going to be court-martialled. He had been sent to take my statement but I was not obliged to say anything. I asked him how they knew there had been thefts. From the inventory, he told me. But, I informed him, I had refused to sign the inventory. That was his first surprise. I then asked if he had seen my report. What report? I suggested we adjourn until he had read it. We met again the next day, in a markedly changed atmosphere. Somebody, he assured me, had been trying to set me up. However there was still a problem, because weapons and ammunition were missing and I had been one of the officers in charge of a guard detail. I shouldn't worry too much about the court martial, but I would probably have to be charged along with various other people. He then went on to tell me some scuttlebutt about our former quartermaster, Louis Hall, who seemed to have gone a step too far in one of his private enterprises, being saved from prosecution only by a mysterious theft of papers from the JAG's offices in Singapore.

The possibility of being detained indefinitely in Malaya to rebut some trumped-up charge was not an agreeable one. There were at that time three kinds of demobilization: Class A, which was when your age and service group came up, being an amalgam of the time you had been in the forces and your age, Class C, or compassionate, usually if your wife was pregnant by another man, and Class B, which was available to those possessed of a qualification or skill which was urgently needed for the United Kingdom economy. Presumably as a method of controlling the ingress to universities after six years, during which those who would have been undergraduates had been serving in the forces, the government had decided to place all those who had won open awards to Cambridge or Oxford universities in Class B, which meant that four of us were due to be sent home in August, to start the university year in October. That was a boat I did not wish to miss.

Martin Gregson, our second-in-command, sent for me, having obviously been briefed about the caves fiasco by the officer from the JAG's department. He was, he told me, about to take command of a regiment in Palestine, and would like me to accompany him as his adjutant, with immediate promotion to the rank of captain. We would be leaving for India very shortly and the matter of the caves would be forgotten. I would however have to sign on for another three years but, he was sure that, in any event, I would not want to leave the army in which I had a glittering future. And more of the same. Thanking him for his confidence and so on, I said I expected to be on my way home within two or three weeks, as I, along with a few others, had been notified we were to travel from Singapore on the *Mauritania*, which was due to sail then. I had enjoyed my years in the army, and the regiment especially, but I did not want to make it my career. It was a reply he had anticipated. 'I don't want you to wait for the *Mauritania*,' he told me. 'The *Monarch of Bermuda* is sailing a week earlier. I want you to catch that. The sooner you are out of South-East Asia Command, the better.' So it was that, while my friends Tony Besch, Michael Gover, and others travelled home together on the *Mauritania*, I left a few days earlier on the *Monarch of Bermuda*. It was galling when they, in the faster liner, passed us in the Red Sea.

It is not easy for those who have lived only in peacetime to comprehend the dislocation to family life caused by a world war lasting more than six years, even in a country like England which had been bombed but not fought over. My father and brother served in the Royal Air Force, and my elder sister had been a meteorological officer in the women's air force, the WAAF. My younger sister had, in 1939, been sent out of danger from bombing and from 1940, after my father rejoined the services, my mother had worked full-time managing his business. One way or another, most families didn't see much of each other during the war, and there was always the worry that one of us would not survive, although I reckon I came closer to being killed while being bombed as a civilian than I ever did in the forces.

Anticipating my homecoming with an enthusiasm engendered by this disruption to family life (although our experience was no different from that of millions of others and we had the good fortune that we all survived), I wired when I left Singapore giving my expected time of arrival in Liverpool, and confirmed it from Port Said. At Gibraltar I received a telegram from my parents saying that the chance of a short holiday in Belgium had come up. They were taking my younger sister with them, but would be back three days after I got home.

The family dog was glad to see me back. When I called from outside the locked house, she wet the floor in her excitement.

I visited Singapore a few times on business after the war but I have never returned to Malaysia. My memories are still of the country as it was six decades ago, whereas I now recall Singapore as another Toronto, Milan, Barcelona, or St Louis: a modern city with the same traffic and airport and cuisine and hotels and crowds of people. Most of my friends in the Royal Devon Yeomanry have been back, and they tell me what a lovely country Malaysia still is, and how friendly its inhabitants are. Perhaps I should make the journey before it is too late. Malaya, as it was then, was very good to us during those eleven months, and I like to think that the Royal Devon Yeomanry was good for Malaya.

12

What Happened Afterwards

TO MALAYSIA

The British Military Administration (BMA) came to an end in April 1946. As this account is no more than the personal memoir of one who played a peripheral role during its existence, the fact that the BMA impinged not at all on my activities cannot be taken as proof that its officials, whoever they were, were not influential in other respects. A letter written to Frank Ellen on 15 December 1945, by a farmer from Ulu Ringlet reported: 'Am still battling with the B.M.A. authorities over the status of this Farm. I deny them the right to call it Relief work, when a Mil. Hospital is supplied with Fresh Milk from Civilian owned cows. But B. M. A. stands for B—— Meddlers All (well nearly) or Black Market Association.' The farmer, whose imprisonment by the Japanese had not blunted his nib, seemed also to have had some unfortunate experiences with Indian officers. After some scandalous generalizations he added: 'Please have a look around the second hand bookshops in Ipoh, whether you can find a copy of Edgar Wallace "The Twister". I need it to present to the Indian Lt Col, in charge of the Mil. Hosp here. May be he can pick up a few tips.'

His comments on the differences between the Japanese and the British are not unexpected but are still worth recording: 'When asked to give a comparison between the Jap. soldiers and the British, just after our release, I answered that one Jap. soldier is a rotter, two are bastards (there was no lady present), three are an Army, Navy and Air Force plus a Gestapo. One British soldier—a Gentleman, Two—God's Own, Three—the Salt of the Earth, And the Fox troop has my first love.' Frank Ellen commanded Fox Troop. The farmer's judgment may have been influenced by a supply of rum Frank had given him.

Another wrong impression I formed at the time was that the opposition to the Japanese had come exclusively from Chinese communists aided by the British Force 136. I now know that during the Japanese occupation there was also the Malay *Tentera Wataniah* (Patriotic Army) and the *Askar Melayu Setia* (Loyal Malay Army) which had the support of the Sultan of Pahang. Even in the MPAJA, not everyone was a communist, a notable exception being the Perak heroine, Sybil Kathigasu, who was awarded the George Medal for bravery. However, following the reoccupation by the British, the communist subversives were predominantly Chinese, with some Indian supporters, but no Malays.

Before the war ended, the Colonial Office in London had hatched plans for a colonial Malayan Union ruled by a British governor, a constitutional change which not only repudiated the various treaties between the British and the Malay Rulers but offended the great mass of the population which wished at the very least to retain their former self-rule under British suzerainty. The formation of the United Malays Nationalist Federation of Malaya in March 1946 under the guidance of the

Ruler of Johore, a state which had always retained its independence, provided a body able to negotiate with the British on behalf of the whole country and all races. At this stage, the communists still had plans to seize power but the main plank of their support, the agitation for the creation of an independent state, was weakened in February 1948, when the Federation of Malaya came into being.

For the next twelve years, with varying degrees of intensity, the fight continued against communist subversion and banditry. The first murders, of three expatriate planters, took place on my old patch on 16 June 1948, their bodies being buried in Batu Gajah. This led to the declaration of a State of Emergency; hence the term 'the Emergency' used to describe the pitiless and bloody struggle which ensued. Newly formed units of the Malay Regiment were attacked as ruthlessly as were Commonwealth troops and by May 1950, the number of serious incidents occasioned by communist activity had risen to 400 a month. Nor was their campaign against civilians solely directed at British expatriates. That year, for less than 1,000 communists captured, surrendered, or killed, government forces lost 1,778 men (killed or wounded) and in addition there were 1,161 civilian casualties.

In 1951, with the killing of non-European civilians especially proving counter-productive, the communists concentrated their attacks on the army, the police, and senior civil servants. The tide turned slowly, aided by the arrival of General Templar as army commander, the reorganization of the police under the guidance of Colonel Young, who was seconded for a year from the City of London police, and the involvement of former members of Force 136. As we had learned five years earlier, the biggest handicap to any fight against terrorism or subversion is the difficulty in gathering information, and the authorities slowly and painfully developed an intelligence service. Other drastic measures included the relocation of villages bordering the jungle to cut off supplies to the rebels, the rationing of food so that villagers had no surplus provisions to hand over to the communists in the jungle, and the introduction of identity cards.

In 1955 the Alliance Party won 51 out of 52 seats in the Federal elections and in August, Tunku Abdul Rahman became Chief Minister in the new government as well as Chairman of the Emergency Operations Council. His attempt to end the war with the communists by negotiation failed and that November they resumed their offensive by an attack in the Cameron Highlands. In 1956, talks took place between the Tunku and the British government which were to lead to full independence. The great day arrived on 31 August 1957, an event which did nothing to diminish the support given to the Malaysian police and army by British, Australian, New Zealand, Rhodesian, Fijian, and Gurkha troops. It would be another three years before the communists were driven out of Malaya into the jungles of southern Thailand, and the cells of the Min Yuen penetrated and broken up, and their control of the trade unions ended.

The Emergency officially ended on 31 July 1960 when the Regulations were repealed. The communists committed sporadic outrages in later years, such as when the Perak Chief of Police was assassinated in 1975. Their final admission of defeat came at a ceremony in southern Thailand when, on 2 December 1989, their leader signed an agreement with the Malaysian government to the effect that hostilities were ended.

Communism was defeated in Malaysia by the granting and gaining of full independence, by the courage and resolution of the Malay army and police aided by the local men serving in the Home Guards, by the help afforded them by Commonwealth troops before and after August 1957, and by the lack of popular support for the rebellion except under duress. The establishment of a prosperous multi-racial state progressively created an environment in which totalitarian Marxism could not put down any roots. Those who were sent from abroad to serve in Malaysia can also take pride in the society which has evolved, however small their own contribution to its success. Before the war, British politicians had long recognized that empire can only be sustained with the acquiescence or consent of the majority of the subject people. After the war, popular support within the United Kingdom for colonialism had evaporated with the return of servicemen who had seen it at first hand. If nothing else, the former imperialists bequeathed to their possessions the invaluable gift of the English language, and, in Malaysia and elsewhere, parted company in a spirit of friendship.

TO THE ROYAL DEVON YEOMEN

Greig Barr, the regiment's commanding officer, returned to Oxford on demobilization and was appointed Sub-rector of Exeter College. In due time he became Rector (or Master) of the College, a Pro-Vice-Chancellor of the University, and a Delegate, or director, of the Oxford University Press. He was also an important figure in the world of academia, as well as in that of rugby. He retained his life-long preference for golf over horse-racing.

David Scott, the 382 Battery Commander and successor to Greig Barr as commanding officer, after the war decided to join the Bar rather than remain a solicitor. He practised on the Western Circuit until increasing deafness, the curse of artillerymen who had no ear protection in those days, caused his premature retirement. He remained a keen follower of the horses, although he was never again appointed a handicapper.

Robert Hudson, who briefly took over command from David Scott, became a cricket commentator, broadcaster, and author. He was also appointed Head of Outside Broadcasting by the BBC.

Frank Ellen, the popular commander of 'F' Troop, became a farmer in Ireland and then worked in the oil industry in the United Kingdom. He married one of the girls at the abortive camp set up to receive the refugees who never arrived from Normandy (apart from the goat).

Glyn Gabe, another respected troop commander who

had helped re-establish latex production, became chief surveyor responsible for the management of the significant estates in South Wales belonging to the Duke of Beaufort.

Philip Shimwell, the gun position officer who, with me, shared responsibility for shelling our own observation post with Greig Barr in it, worked in the shipping business in Bristol before becoming proprietor of a leading company of international tug-brokers in London.

Gordon Samuels, a troop commander and magistrate, returned to Australia where he became a High Court judge and Governor General of New South Wales. A planned stay with Glyn Gabe in Wales had to be postponed when he received an invitation from the Queen to be her guest at Balmoral.

As for the two educationalists: **Geoff Stavert** joined the Royal Navy as a teacher and, at last sighting, was a Commander RN. **Neil McGill** also went back to teaching in his native Scotland.

Frank Bedder, who worked with local bankers in Ipoh and ran the Tote, became managing director of a large clothing business in Leicester. I last saw him in the early 1980s at a company Annual General Meeting in London when a stranger approached me with the words, 'I'm Frank.' It took a few seconds for the penny to drop. As a shareholder he had noticed that I was on the board and had travelled down to see me.

Maurice Swain, the clerk of the course at the Boxing Day races, became a high-class antique dealer in London and was last sighted in Mayfair wearing a bowler hat and carrying an umbrella.

Bill Noon, the assistant adjutant whose presence in brigade headquarters at Tapah facilitated the re-allotment of unwanted supplies of rum, became the proprietor of a business concentrating on reclaiming and refining oil.

John Jones, described by his battery commander John Hassall as the best subaltern he had known, joined the colonial civil service in Sudan before being transferred to intelligence. He retired as head of MI5, the British Intelligence Services. In that position he advised Mrs Thatcher to ignore the Spycatcher book being published in Australia by Peter Wright on the grounds that it had all been said before by Chapman Pincher and it would be stupid to give any publicity to an eccentric figure such as Wright. She should have listened to him.

Michael Shorter, my fellow survivor as a lieutenant in 382 Battery, became a Professor of Philosophy in Oxford. As Greig Barr remarked, he clearly learned something from his association with us. I cannot report whether or not he persisted with the clarinet and I have not heard his name mentioned in musical circles.

Michael Gover, another lieutenant, from 469 Battery, also settled in Oxford, becoming headmaster of the Dragon School, the leading preparatory school, and concerning himself with rugby administration.

Desmond Mangham, who led in the first winner at

Ipoh, stayed in the army and retired as a Major-General. He then secured a plum job, becoming Director of the Brewers' Society.

Reg Ferguson, the smiling adjutant whose kind suggestion that I should recover the padre's jeep so that I could see my brother was typical of his consideration for other people regardless of rank, worked in the insurance industry. After retirement he used the same skills as a voluntary bursar in the Leonard Cheshire/Sue Ryder Foundations. He was also godfather to Frank Ellen's daughter.

Tony Besch of 469 Battery, later known as Anthony, was director of the Oxford University Dramatic Society before becoming a leading figure in the theatrical and operatic world, being for many years associated with the world-famous Glyndebourne Music Festival. He tried to educate me culturally when we spent a week together in Paris over Easter, 1947, by taking me twice to the opera and once to see Jean-Louis Barrault in *Hamlet*. In return I took him to the Folies Bergères. (In the light of the current debate over student fees, it may be worth noting that our total expenses for the week, including our fares, hotel bills, meals, and so on, came to just under £10. Our student grant, net of tuition fees and the cost of books, was £300 a year.) In later years a young friend, who is an opera singer, was amazed to hear that someone as uncouth as me had been a friend and companion of the legendary Anthony Besch.

Alan Maidens, whose demobilization was delayed until 1947, joined his family's garage business in Croydon and built it up to a substantial concern with four main car distributorships.

Our medical officer, **Tegwyn Jones**, was a general practitioner in Cardiff and our signaller, **Robert Steven**, became managing director of a leading company of insurance brokers in London. I met Robert quite often over the years as three of the firms I worked for used their services.

As for the regular soldiers, **Martin Gregson** remained active in the racing world in which he became a leading figure in the west-country. **Louis Hall**, the quartermaster, left Malaya without a stain on his character. Given the task of raising a gun to the top of the tall and hollow Shot Tower at the Festival of Britain in 1951, he contrived to let it fall down the middle, which did no good either to his military career or to the ordnance.

My last encounter with Trussy, battery **Sergeant Major Truscott**, was long ago when I was taking a train from Kingsbridge up the branch line to South Brent, to catch the express to London. The train stopped a little short of the platform and then pulled forward. When we halted again, Trussy, the engine-driver, was waiting at the door, having handed over his duties to his fireman. He said he had spied me from his cab as I boarded the train. He insisted on carrying my bag across the bridge to the main line and then seeing me into my compartment, to the surprise of the other occupants.

I met **Corporal Jenkins** when I was playing cricket for Kingsbridge at Babbacombe just after the war and he was watching the game. Not disgracing the regiment, I had managed to score a modest twenty-five runs. I am sure that **John Hassall**, who had become a leading hotelier in neighbouring Torquay, knew enough not to employ Mr Jenkins in his kitchens, unless of course the menu included tinned fish.

Of the other characters, **Gunners Love** and **Tripp**, **Bombardier Twentyman**, **Lance-Bombardier Hornsby**, **Sergeant Peasey**, and **ASM Major**, I have no news. I am sure that they too prospered in civilian life as I know did other officers in the regiment whose names have not appeared in my story.

There may still be lessons to be learned as to why it was that young men, not just in the regiment but throughout the services, adjusted effortlessly to civilian life after years in uniform, and nearly all prospered. They had benefited from the discipline, from their early financial independence, and from exercising responsibility at a relatively young age. Another important factor was illustrated by a trivial event in the dire winter of 1946, which was especially unpleasant for those who had been living in the tropics. I had met a friend for the evening in London and, after seeing her home, arrived at Liverpool Street station long after my last train had left. I therefore caught another which stopped at a junction some fifteen miles short of where I wanted to go. When we arrived, the platform was deserted and so I strolled up the line to the signal box, where the signalmen kindly stopped a light engine (one on its own), which was going in my direction. The driver gave me a lift on the footplate, not just to my station, but to a bridge beyond it three hundred yards from my parents' home. The next morning my father said, 'You can't do things like that.' But we could. And most of us did. We had learned that every problem has a solution but, if you can't do anything about it, stop worrying.

TO THE OPEL

In the summer of 1948, I met someone who had been living in Penang. I asked her if she had seen an Opel two-door coupé with a left-hand drive on the island. She told me it was owned by the harbourmaster, who was very proud of it.

Glossary

ASM	Artificer Sergeant Major, the senior non-commissioned officer in the REME.
BBC	British Broadcasting Corporation.
BMA	British Military Administration, the body which governed Malaya from September 1945 to April 1946.
DUKW	A large amphibious vehicle also known as a Duck. The acronym designates the design specification.
Force 136	The special troops of the 14th Army operating behind enemy lines.
INA	The Indian National Army, a unit raised by the Japanese from prisoners-of-war and local volunteers.
LAD	Light Aid Detachment, the REME unit stationed in an artillery regiment.
JAG	Judge-Advocate General, an army's senior lawyer.
JIFF	A member of the Indian National Army, or Japanese/Indian Freedom Fighter.
MPAJA	Malayan People's Anti-Japanese Army, a mainly Chinese communist body aided by Force 136.
OCTU	Officer Cadet Training Unit.
RAF	Royal Air Force.
RDY	Royal Devon Yeomanry—96th Field Regiment Royal Artillery, originally a Territorial unit raised in Newton Abbot, Torquay, and Totnes in South Devon.
REME	Royal Electrical and Mechanical Engineers—technicians who were also attached to service units.
RN	Royal Navy.
SEAC	South-East Asia Command. It was also the name of the Forces' newspaper.
SS	Nazi protection squads (Schutzstaffeln).
WAAF	Women's Auxiliary Air Force.
Wren	A member of the Women's Royal Naval Service.

Further Reading

Japan's Imperial Conspiracy by David Bergamini tells the story of Japanese aggression from its beginning with the seizure of Mukden in 1931 until the surrender to the Allies in 1945. For the emperor's role, see *Hirohito: Behind the Myth* by Edward Behr.

For the invasion of Malaya and the fall of Singapore, see the full account in Liddell Hart's *History of the Second World War* and John Keegan's absorbing *The Second World War*. Dato' H.L. (Mike) Wrigglesworth's *The Japanese Invasion of Kelantan in 1941* gives valuable detailed information.

The role of the British/Indian 14th Army is superbly told by Sir William Slim in *Defeat into Victory*. His *Unofficial History* dealing with his other campaigns is equally enthralling and deserves to be more widely known. For what it was like to be a young conscript in Slim's army, read *Quartered Safe Out Here* by George MacDonald Fraser (of Flashman fame). It has been described as the best memoir of the Second World War to have been written by any soldier.

For an Australian serviceman's description of the fighting in Malaya in 1941 and 1942 see *You'll Die in Singapore* by Charles McCormac.

Among the many books written about the ordeal of prisoners taken by the Japanese, see *The War Diaries of Weary Dunlop*, *The Railway Man* by Eric Lomax, *The Naked Island* by Russell Braddon, *Escape into Captivity* by Peter Hartley, and *Ordeal by Endurance* by Donald C. Eyre.

The mysterious abortive attack on Phuket is described in *Code Breaker in the Far East* by Alan Stripp. F. Spencer Chapman's *The Jungle is Neutral*, describing his years as a fugitive in Japanese-occupied Malaya, deserves re-reading.

Further information on the war crimes trials can be learned from *Victor's Justice: The Tokyo War Crimes Trial* by the appropriately named R.H. Victor.

To learn what happened in Malaya during the period of the civil war against the Communists, the 'Emergency', see Yuen Yuet Leng's *Operation Ginger* and R. Thambipillay's two books, *God's Little Acre 1948–1998* and *The Malayan Police Force in the Emergency 1948–1960*.